Cut Out

Also available

Being Red
A Politics for the Future
Ken Livingstone

Syriza
Inside the Labyrinth
Kevin Ovenden
Foreword by Paul Mason

The Rent Trap
How We Fell Into It and How We Get Out of It
Rosie Walker and Samir Jeraj

Cut Out

Living Without Welfare

Jeremy Seabrook

PlutoPress
www.plutobooks.com

To Barrie Blower, in homage and friendship.

First published 2016 by Pluto Press
345 Archway Road, London N6 5AA

www.plutobooks.com

Copyright © Jeremy Seabrook 2016

The right of Jeremy Seabrook to be identified as the author of this work
has been asserted by him in accordance with the Copyright, Designs and
Patents Act 1988.

The Left Book Club, founded in 2014, company number 9338285
pays homage to the original Left Book Club founded by Victor Gollancz
in 1936.

British Library Cataloguing in Publication Data
A catalogue record for this book is available from the British Library

ISBN   978 0 7453 3618 3   Paperback
ISBN   978 1 7837 1803 0   PDF eBook
ISBN   978 1 7837 1805 4   Kindle eBook
ISBN   978 1 7837 1804 7   EPUB eBook

This book is printed on paper suitable for recycling and made from fully
managed and sustained forest sources. Logging, pulping and manufacturing
processes are expected to conform to the environmental standards of the
country of origin.

Typeset by Stanford DTP Services, Northampton, England

Simultaneously printed in the European Union and United States of America

Contents

Series preface

The first Left Book Club (1936–48) had 57,000 members, had distributed 2 million books, and had formed 1,200 workplace and local groups by the time it peaked in 1939. LBC members were active throughout the labour and radical movement at the time, and the Club became an educational mass movement, remodelling British public opinion and contributing substantially to the Labour landslide of 1945 and the construction of the welfare state.

Publisher Victor Gollancz, the driving force, saw the LBC as a movement against poverty, fascism, and the growing threat of war. He aimed to resist the tide of austerity and appeasement, and to present radical ideas for progressive social change in the interests of working people. The Club was about enlightenment, empowerment, and collective organisation.

The world today faces a crisis on the scale of the 1930s. Capitalism is trapped in a long-term crisis. Financialisation and austerity are shrinking demand, deepening the depression, and widening social inequalities. The social fabric is being torn apart. International relations are increasingly tense and militarised. War threatens on several fronts, while fascist and racist organisations are gaining ground across much of Europe. Global warming threatens the planet and the whole of humanity with climate catastrophe. Workplace organisation has been weakened, and social democratic parties have been hollowed out by acceptance of pro-market dogma. Society has become more atomised, and mainstream politics suffers an acute democratic deficit.

Yet the last decade has seen historically unprecedented levels of participation in street protest, implying a mass audience for radical alternatives. But socialist ideas are no longer, as in the immediate post-war period, 'in the tea'. One of neoliberalism's achievements has been to undermine ideas of solidarity, collective provision, and public service.

The Left Book Club aspires to meet the ideological challenge posed by the global crisis. Our aim is to offer high-quality books at affordable prices that are carefully selected to address the central issues of the day and to be accessible to a wide general audience. Our list represents the full range of progressive traditions, perspectives, and ideas. We hope the books will be used as the basis of reading circles, discussion groups, and other educational and cultural activities relevant to developing, sharing, and disseminating ideas for radical change in the interests of the common people at home and abroad.

The Left Book Club collective

Acknowledgements

I would like to thank all the people in the West Midlands who have helped with this book for their kind contributions.

Jeremy Seabrook
2016

...those whom God doth punishe with povertie, let no man seeke to oppresse with crueltie

—An Ease for Overseers of the Poore,
published anonymously in Cambridge, 1601

Introduction

'Rich' and 'poor' are ancient, apparently inseparable opposites; sometimes antagonistic (the rich monopolise the necessities of the poor), at others symbiotic (without the wealth-creators we cannot afford the social amenities we need). The words are so clear, and so deeply embedded in linguistic habit, that we have almost ceased to ask how people come to be included in these categories: they are self-evident, unavoidable. The rich, like the poor in scriptural admonition, will always be with us.

This book is concerned with what makes people poor in modern societies, and what prompts governments to relieve or to aggravate poverty. The economic condition of 'the poor' – an abstract collective noun – has been the object of much attention throughout history, not least because of their capacity to disrupt or interfere with the established order. Their social and political potential for mischief has been a matter of great concern to ruling elites. They have been in receipt of both punishment and leniency, according to the temper of the age. It might have been thought that in countries as rich as ours, the poor would be treated with consideration, if not tenderness. This is far from being the case.

The condition of poor people in societies of unparalleled wealth raises certain questions. Since most people in Europe, North America and Australia are no longer poor, those who remain so have become victims of a popular contempt that was absent when a majority of the people lived in poverty. (What the wealthy minority thought about them is another matter, since they have been constantly referred to in disparaging terms – the great unwashed, the masses, the hoi polloi, the common people; more recently, the underclass, trailer trash, losers.)

'The poor' have been only crudely differentiated, usually into groups understood to be meritorious or culpable, that is, deserving and undeserving. Much effort has been expended on defining the virtuous poor by ascribing exculpatory causes to their poverty. Everyone knows that widows and orphans, the lame, halt and blind may be poor through no fault of their own; while the idle and vicious, the feckless and addicted, the degenerate and improvident are thrown into the category of the perverse and wilful. If an aura of piety surrounds the idea of the blameless poor, denunciations of those who have brought upon themselves their own misfortune are far more resonant and morally charged. There is something satisfying in the condemnation by the righteous of those they see as unworthy and excluded. And a minoritised poor – welfare cheats, scroungers, skivers, parasites, free-loaders, beggars – attract a lexicon of abuse in rich societies, in which majorities no longer insecure can congratulate themselves on their own (often less than merited) prosperity, while expressing their loathing for those unable, for whatever reason, to avail themselves of the abundance which developed societies have placed, at least in theory, within the reach of everyone.

The economic function of the poor in our time is twofold. They serve first of all as a constant reminder that yet more economic growth is essential in order to remedy their plight and to lessen their – already diminished – numbers; and secondly as a spur to further self-enrichment by those who have already achieved much, since to fall into poverty is a fate not to be contemplated. Poverty must remain grim, a state to be dreaded. For this reason, poverty in the contemporary rich world has a strong element of contrivance: it must remain as a deterrent, in order to encourage the respectable and the well-to-do to avoid it all costs.

There is clearly a contradiction in these purposes: piety is at war with condemnation. This is not difficult to explain – the 'need' for constant economic expansion must be maintained, since this is the vital purpose of the economic system itself; yet this increasing plenty must still exclude significant cohorts of people, in order that they may be brandished as a scarecrow at those comfortably situated. In other words, the poor must be punished, but they must on no account be permitted to vanish, for their presence is essential: to be scourged, but not into disappearance.

This dual function makes for a certain complexity – ensuring poverty-abatement but not poverty-elimination is quite a tricky task in an economy that produces annually some £2 trillion in GDP. But remarkably effective ways have been found to ensure that enough people remain poor, or on the verge of poverty, to prevent the rest of us from becoming complacent or, even worse, admitting that we have enough for our needs; such an admission would, of course, be catastrophic for an economy which depends upon a perception of perpetual scarcity in order to keep on expanding.

This book tries to show how certain individuals remain or become poor; and also to account for efforts by the present government to impoverish them further, in the interests of maintaining a sense of insecurity among the better-off. 'Reforms' to the welfare system should be seen in this light; for they ensure that poverty – as a carefully maintained and harrowing experience – is in no danger of being eradicated, and that the poor, unlike many other creatures in the world, are in little imminent danger of becoming an extinct species.

The 'causes' of poverty may be sought primarily, not in the easy moral categories beloved by politicians, but in the profound inequalities that are part of the great diversity of human characteristics. It is difficult to ascribe individual responsibility to the existence of such a distribution, which is why we tend to concentrate solely on *behaviour*, to which everyone is expected to conform, despite their differences in endowment, inheritance and capacity. Some cultures, of course, value certain human attributes above others; but, in general, a particular set of observances, decencies and codes of conduct is exacted in all societies. Those which prevail in our privileged moment make it rare indeed for people to make a virtue of restraint, frugality and abstention from consuming as much as human beings can when they set their minds and money to it.

While researching this book, I was struck by the factors, some profound and ineradicable, some easily remediable, which had determined the state of want and lack of basic necessities in the lives of people who might appear as failures, as unsuccessful, poor or marginalised; and by how little of this complex skein of circumstances could be reasonably interpreted as a result of their own wilful behaviour. Who, with any other option, actually makes a 'choice' to sit in the rain or under a bridge stinking of piss, holding out a styrofoam cup to receive pence from passers-by?

In the judgements and condemnations lie archaic remnants of morality long overtaken by what we now know about human psychology, the nature of societies, and the inheritance of individuals. Is it an absence of imagination, an inability to enter into the experience of others, or a residual conviction in the existence of an unqualified 'free will' that makes us humiliate poor people? It is a constant refrain of the successful that 'If I could rise out of poverty and disadvantage to become what I am today, why can't he or she?' The argument suggests that because some people have been able to make good in the world, despite the most horrific circumstances of birth and upbringing, it must follow that if others fail to do the same, they are in some way guilty and must be stigmatised accordingly. Rather than singing hymns of gratitude to their good fortune, those who have risen in the world often prefer to turn indignantly upon those incapable of following the path they have 'chosen', and to condemn their inability to do so as a moral failure.

The wounds and injuries suffered by many poor people do not enter into the crude calculus by which benefit systems, social security arrangements or welfare provisions operate. Yet if anything close to 'social justice' were to be established, it would be necessary to inquire into the situation of those disadvantaged a) psychologically (lovelessness or bereavement, neglect or cruelty in childhood), b) intellectually (people endowed with a modest capacity for reasoning), c) socially (the inheritance of generations of servitude or slavery), d) mentally (the chance distribution of emotional and psychiatric disorders), e) linguistically (those in a society they do not understand), f) culturally (people whose traditions and norms are at odds with the dominant social values), g) genetically (inherited diseases and health conditions, including some very common ailments, prone to heart disease and cancer), h) accidentally (victims of traffic or other accidents), i) traumatically (especially through war, crime or natural catastrophe), or j) randomly (as in the distribution of certain characteristics, such as timidity, fear, anxiety or recklessness). Many other human features readily stigmatised – idleness, promiscuity, irresponsibility, anger – were not actively selected by those who exhibit them. And this takes no account of the predictable trajectory of human lives – the dependency of childhood, the ability to procure and sustain labour that will provide a living, the process of ageing, decline and death.

It was an awareness of these complexities that informed the basic premise of the welfare state: to answer need at the point where it was identified, irrespective of the cause. 'Need' is no more enhanced by virtue than it is cancelled by unworthiness. The provision of welfare was originally against the known vicissitudes of human life, and broadly, against the vagaries of economic cycles – times of full employment, of recession, of economic change, of the impoverishment of some groups and the prosperity of others. It was a fairly blunt instrument, but the misfortunes to which all humanity is prey at one time or another endowed it with a sense of fairness and propriety, recognised and approved of by a majority.

If the subsequent partial privatisation of provision for unemployment and old age, as well as private health insurance and education services, the raising of fees for university education, the necessity for the individual to make his or her accommodation with a capitalism become global, have combined to make the idea of a welfare state appear as redundant as many of those to whose afflictions it was designed to respond, the biggest contributor to its apparent dispensability has been the growth in prosperity and the rise in living standards. This has made a majority feel secure in providing for their own needs (with the exception of the National Health

Service, which remains one of the most loved institutions in Britain, the erosion of which is both feared and resented), and has created a sense of daily well-being for a majority who do not foresee long periods of dependency upon State support. This, together with the spectre of spiralling 'welfare costs', has made possible the government assault on the well-being of poor people, with only modest resistance from the still-prosperous majority, who, confident that they will not fall into want, often feel distant and uninvolved in the fate of the unfortunate. 'There but for the grace of God go I' was a common reaction at a time of mass insecurity and poverty; but as we have become richer, the grace of God has become, like the finances required by welfare, a scarce resource, and we need no longer look with the same compassion upon those in whose wounded lives we might once have been able to read our own possible destiny.

It cannot be a lack of resources that prompts cuts in welfare in a country which, despite the recent recession, has never been richer, and in which a potlatch of excess co-exists with a pinched, skinny misery. If a country virtually bankrupted by the Second World War could find the wherewithal to institute a universal welfare system, the claim in that same country, awash with luxury, ostentation and extravagance, that it can no longer afford to care for its least fortunate is so blatant an untruth as scarcely to need refutation. If public anger against government policy has been muted, this is probably because the actions of government are seen by the poor as simply yet another malignant visitation among many, as part of the bleak landscape of the deprivation they have come to expect in life.

There are two obvious tasks facing today's dissenters and radicals, although the fact that they are self-evident does not make their accomplishment any easier. These are not the overthrow of capitalism (of which there seems little chance), and certainly not acceptance of the current 'reforms', which is a euphemism for the undermining of welfare. The first is to strive for greater fairness, in which the wealthiest will make a just contribution to the well-being of those out of whose labour, acquiescence and powerlessness their fortunes are made; the second is to embark on a genuine reform of welfare, which will provide the damaged and injured of capitalism with a decent subsistence that does not debar them from full participation in the life of society, however eccentric and wasteful that society may have become.

Such feasible improvements demand a more humane understanding of the needs of the vulnerable and deprived; the more so since many of those vulnerabilities and deprivations have been artfully and cunningly wrought, in order to maintain poverty rather than to alleviate it. As it is, personnel administering the benefits system are themselves undervalued in an unequal society, and the low worth in which they are held gives them an added inducement to visit their own resentment upon those they are supposed to serve. More sensitive training and appreciation of the life of people who use all welfare services should be instituted. A more responsive approach to 'casework' by the social work profession (itself also discredited in our baleful, welfare-hating age), should be available, and assessments of need not left to a mechanistic calculus, the justice of which few are in a position to monitor. Assessing the needs of other human beings is not an ignoble undertaking, the drudgery of ill-paid functionaries. It should be endowed with prestige and a sense of 'vocation' (that curious word which meant 'calling', not necessarily by God, but by the heart and imagination, themselves now atrophied organs in a dust-dry system increasingly void of compassion). A renewal and re-dedication of the welfare state is on few political agendas; probably because it is the first requirement of a regenerated humane society. That political parties vie with each other in denouncing the poor, and in pleading the artificial poverty that prevents the richest societies in history from assisting those in need, should be denounced for the cant that it is.

The thrust of the present Conservative 'reforms' to the welfare system has deep historic roots, and they are the opposite of what is required to bring relief to the poor. It imposes an ideological rigour that stifles and conceals real needs. The 'discipline' of reduced incomes, the sanctioning of benefits, the withdrawal of support, evoke an old and – it had been thought – discredited tradition of compulsion enshrined in centuries of punitive poor laws, workhouses and all the other instruments and institutions of 'correction' for those spectres at the feast of wealth and power, who, if excluded from it, were obliged to serve it with mute and subservient respect.

There are two main themes addressed in this book: first, the personal, social and psychological forces that contribute to contemporary poverty; and second, the failure of those who have the capacity to do so to offer any useful or plausible remedy other than their own prejudices. That this latter process has so far worked better than the government might have expected – with relative social peace and the easy crushing of dissent – does not mean that such a happy situation will last for ever. The direction in which capitalism is moving – as Oxfam reveals that the richest 62 people on the planet own as much wealth as the poorest half of humanity – does not suggest that the poor will remain for ever quiescent, or even in a permanent minority. Pressure on new generations, the degradation of work, the insecurity and fragility of general prosperity, the accumulation of private debt, long-term stagnation of incomes, the disparagement of public sector workers, homelessness, people being forced to work at levels far below their capacity, the unstoppable growth of inequality – all this scarcely confirms the picture of progress the government paints, any more than it supports its vision of a 'high-wage, low-welfare, low-tax' economy. Poverty, in societies of such wealth, is economic violence – a phenomenon that goes unrecognised as such because 'economic forces' (with their coercive overtones) are noted for their impersonal nature, their capacity to deprive by stealth, so that impoverishment appears as a 'natural' phenomenon.

Patience and resignation have always been commended to the dispossessed by those who have withheld from them, or robbed them of, a decent sufficiency. And for long periods they have shown acquiescence and fortitude. But such qualities, admirable though they may be, are not inexhaustible. Sooner or later, they will rise up to instruct ruling elites, rarely with the magisterial loftiness with which they have themselves been treated, in the necessity for greater humanity and forbearance.

The sudden awakening of the much paraded (but for the past six years at least, slumbering) social conscience of Iain Duncan Smith, and his resignation from government in March 2016, undermined the principal pillar of Conservative social policy, and admitted to the world that its devotion to austerity is elective. He confirmed the story of this book, and what many have long suspected – that 'reform' of the welfare state is simply a euphemism for demolition.

Jeremy Seabrook
March 2016

Welfare cuts: the wider context

The welfare state was the supreme achievement of decades of popular struggle against poverty, insecurity and squalor. That it should now be subject to a systematic erosion, if not demolition, has troubling implications; for upon it depend many other gains won from an industrial system, into the service of which the people of Britain were pressed two centuries ago. A comprehensive welfare system provided the security on which a wider distribution of wealth and the opportunities that come with it were possible; and out of that enhanced well-being grew a greater tolerance of diversity and acceptance of different identities. These developments, all relatively recent, have been presented as evidence of 'progress' in the capitalist system. One obvious question raised by the attrition of welfare is whether these advantages could *only* occur in capitalist society.

The compensations delivered to the people in the last few decades should be regarded with a certain scepticism. For if capitalism bestowed upon the people the welfare state, with its protections against the social evils of unemployment and poverty and the existential uncertainties of ageing, sickness and loss, it did so only after earlier threats to its survival – the aftermath of a fascism that had convulsed Europe, and the golden promises of a socialism that were to remain unfulfilled. For some time, it was assumed that the welfare state was part of a permanent arrangement. The fact that it represented merely a temporary compromise between capital and labour has only recently begun to dawn upon us, as the representatives of capitalist restoration set about the destruction of that humane institution. George Osborne has declared a new 'settlement' in place – of 'higher wages, lower taxes and lower welfare'. It seems that an economic order which once gave can also now take away. The dissolution of a system dedicated to the health and welfare of the people is described as a withdrawal of 'luxuries we can no longer afford' – in a world that has never been richer.

Because the welfare system is the foundation on which many of the most admired achievements of our society are founded – affluence and the growth in tolerance of different ethnicities, faiths, gender and sexual orientation – it follows that, if social protection can be eroded, nothing else is safe. Without the welfare state, how would economic well-being have been possible? If people had remained prey to the malignancies of nineteenth-century capitalism – malnutrition, disease and misery – the pleasures of plenty would have been tainted, to say the least. The great consumer boom could scarcely have taken place if hunger, dirt and sickness had continued to dominate popular experience.

And later, how would the much-advertised humanitarianism, anti-racism, the rights of women and of lesbians, gay men and transgender people and those with disability, have come about, without the underlying security provided by the apparently happy marriage of welfare with consumerism? The stability that permitted a more liberal society was part of the social edifice which is now being undermined.

The significance of this is startling. It should not be imagined that an inherent love of people of colour, of lesbians and gays, or even of women, lies at the root of capitalist freedoms. These emancipations are recent, opportunistic developments, originally calculated to contrast with the social repressions of the Soviet system. They have served, not principally to liberate those enfranchised by legislation enshrining equality, but primarily to assist capitalism in defining and defending itself against its enemies – and its most implacable enemy now is, of course, Islam, which has taken over from communism, and its predecessor fascism, as the greatest challenge to its supremacy in the world. It is hardly incredible that a system which, with such clamorous self-congratulation, introduced a welfare state to protect the weakest could subsequently pull it apart, that the same system could not annul what we have been encouraged to see as 'irreversible' gains in the social sphere, namely, an abhorrence of racism, a concern for the freedom of women, a commitment to the rights of lesbians, gay men and other minorities.

After all, racism and the subjection of large parts of the world in its name were more than acceptable until the day before yesterday; men were punishable with imprisonment for 'homosexual acts' until the 1960s; and most women lived in forced carceral domesticity until well into the twentieth century. More than this: racism was, as it were, the official doctrine of the high imperial age; and the idea that colonial peoples were 'not ready' for self-government was a tenacious – and violent – conviction among those who resisted the liberation of former colonial possessions. Today's champions of women, ethnic minorities and gays would be less insistent if they did not have in their sights the oppressions of a religious ideology against which to proclaim their credo of liberation. And even among the noisy emancipations of capitalist 'progress', there are always forces eager to undo what they see as the 'mischief' of anti-racism, the infringement of a Christian prohibition on same-sex relationships, and the control by women over their own bodies. Indeed, these forces have already become more strident in this age of contrived 'austerity' which has, miraculously, spared only the rich.

The claim that such emancipatory benefits - now promoted by social and economic arrangements established by elites which, until very recently, expressed either distaste or indifference towards them – are possible only under the benign influence of a capitalist system is a useful political tool with which to belabour repressive and authoritarian regimes around the world. Many of these, of course, also bear the ossified values of a defunct imperialism – oppressive attitudes dumped by colonial powers on other cultures, which they subsequently made their own, even as the imperial entity saw the error of its ways and moved on. One has only to think of the penalties for homosexuality in Uganda, Nigeria and other territories once occupied by Britain; exotic weeds planted by colonialism that took on an autonomous and invasive life of their own. Enlightenment on the evils of patriarchy, same-sex relationships and, above all, racism are very late developments within the Western heartlands; and values which were treated as imperishable truths only one or two generations ago, have been consigned, if not to oblivion, then at least to a provisional forgetting. Languishing in the conserving chambers of memory, they remain available to be dusted down and paraded once more should the ruling elites consider this necessary for their own self-preservation.

If confirmation were needed that 'values' are adopted and discarded according to political expediency, and not because they are inherent in 'our' world-view, we only have to look at the way in which the Soviet Union was regarded by the West in the 1950s and '60s. At that time, among the horror stories about communism frequently aired in the Western media was its failure to make distinctions between men and women: images were broadcast of 'viragos' driving tractors, female labourers on building sites (so different from the pert and pretty images of Hollywood), and offered as evidence of the unsexing power of socialism, while children were consigned to State nurseries soon after birth in order to compel women into the labour force. This was a time when gender stereotypes in the US and Europe were expressed in that staple of early TV adverts, the excited 'housewife' enthusing over some new product, while male breadwinners with creased brows came home after a tiring day at the office to conjugally dutiful wives who set their supper before them and warmed their slippers. With the eclipse of communism, it is as though the 1950s critique of its emancipatory role in women's lives had never occurred, and today we take for granted, as an aspect of our own 'universal' values, what was not so long ago held up as a repelling example of communist 'inhumanity'.

We are also living with other consequences of that earlier political struggle, which have baleful implications for the world. Until the 1960s it remained unclear whether communism would lose out to its capitalist rival, but in the competitive race between them, the mere affluence of the 1950s bloomed into the florid consumerism of later decades. While the Soviet Union could offer its captive peoples only inelegant, malfunctioning goods in the steel-grey landscape of a monochrome socialism, the West dazzled its own people – and the wider world – with the variety and inventiveness of its productive power. This proved to be the most critical guarantor of its victory over its rival. The imagery of abundance and luxury not only assumed a life of its own, but also induced a whole world to 'vote with its feet', seeking out the source of plenty in the great scattering of people of our time. This is also part of the aftermath of that now-forgotten competition between the West and the Soviet Union. Today's refugees, now told that 'the streets of London are not paved with gold' and that Britain is not 'a land of milk and honey', can be excused for their confusion: for the past 40 years they have been the recipients of an imagery depicting in high colour the wealth and comfort of the Western world.

The claim that all the desirable changes we have seen are possible only in capitalist societies is employed to discourage any straying from the path required to maintain them. The 'advances' we have achieved are uniquely a result of our way of life; the road we have taken the only possible road to freedom. There is, of course, always a long way to go. But the admonition is clear: any interference with, or questioning of, the wise values of the settlement under which we live can lead only to loss, breakdown and violence.

These developments have sprung from the continuing growth and expansion of capitalism. They have undoubtedly cleared spaces for previously oppressed people to flourish. The maintenance and further extension of these freedoms allegedly requires continual – indeed, unending – economic growth. This is the basis for the lately achieved liberties, which exist only *within* capitalism's closed world of economic necessity. That world is, however, *not* coterminous with the wider world on which it depends – as the ruinous consequences for the biosphere, the earth and its climate, have now made plain.

The enlargement of liberties within industrial society has incurred costs which do not show up in its accounting system. It is now commonplace to acknowledge that many of the reckonings of economic growth have been externalised, rigorously excluded by the ideological instruments employed by economic reason. Among these, many of the most obvious are rarely out of the news: unstoppable movements of people disturbed by the imperatives of globalism, wars over water, the spread of diseases like Ebola, resource depletion, species extinction, pollution, ocean acidification, and, of course, the global monoculture of consumption, which is not only the fastest-growing cult in the world, but is also raising the temperature of the planet – both physically and socially – to dangerously feverish levels.

The conditions that have produced both social tolerance and global warming are attributable to spectacular economic growth, whereby, through the alchemy of capitalism, prosperity became affluence, affluence became consumerism and consumerism itself has become *consumptive,* a global wasting disease. From the start, the iconography of the good life had a hyperbolic quality; its self-advertisement and anthems to its own capacity for production served a function other than that of answering human needs. That is to say, it was a caricature of what it claimed to be, a deformation of the simple concept of 'sufficiency', which it mocked, since it was not accompanied by a sense of security, but by an urgent desire for more – that imperative of capitalism which, apparently successfully, grafted itself onto human desire and its yearning for transcendence. The resulting hybrid was described as 'human nature', as though all human striving could be answered by the growth and expansion of one economic system.

This is why the time of plenty was also mysteriously accompanied by an obscure sense of penury. It appeared that an ancient craving to secure enough for our sustenance was no longer a realisable or desirable goal. The longing for 'more' was actually not a human aspiration, but a capitalist inspiration: and once that was accepted as the objective of 'progress', no one would ever again be able to define what constituted enough for human contentment. Caught up in an externally generated compulsion towards growth, what was labelled 'human nature' was in effect the nature of an economic system; and many of the pathologies of the modern world stem from this falsification at source of human need, desire and yearning. The rewards, gifts, prizes and freebies showered upon people suggested a newly benevolent capitalism, an apparently spontaneous giving such as the world had never before seen. This might – given the brutal history of industrial society – have alerted us to the idea that certain penalties were lurking beneath the politics of burnished surfaces and the presentational gifts of the masters of public relations.

In other words, the decorative attributes of this version of development – social, economic and human – serve to obscure the great open secret of the 'advanced' world; namely, that the 'laws of economics' are no such thing: they are merely the rules of the only game the rich are prepared to play. Politicians are their proxy players, and any who refuse to observe these conventions are duly declared 'unelectable', as the false sense of crisis generated by Jeremy Corbyn's election as leader of the Labour Party clearly demonstrated.

As welfare is diminished, so other elements of life are compromised – perhaps not dramatically at first (although this can occur with tragic suddenness for those who lose their livelihoods due to illness or other misfortune) but by degrees, insidiously – not least of them, the freedoms implied in the term 'purchasing power'. In the USA, this form of popular potency has virtually stagnated for 40 years (except among the very rich). In Britain, in 2014, the average weekly disposable income was at an eleven-year low, and its recent reversal has been dependent upon a deepening indebtedness of households. The reasons for this are not far to seek: the globalisation of the Western developmental model means that all countries of the world are set in competition with each other, and it becomes necessary for the erstwhile privileged countries (or 'economies' as they are sometimes called) to vie with low-wage entities formerly known as 'underdeveloped'. The implications of this are sometimes described as 'a race to the bottom': a competitive striving to reduce wages and increase productivity at any cost, even if this means maintaining large numbers of people at subsistence levels or below.

In this way, the direction of travel of today's pioneers, these voortrekkers with their heads turned towards the past, becomes plain. Not only are many young people, as well as the expellees of industrial life, the marginal and the demotivated, cut off from the expectations of permanent 'improvement', but even more people are nourishing economic growth with increased personal borrowing and a descent into unpayable debt. At the same time, there has been a fading of what we formerly acknowledged as 'British values' – tolerance, fair play and sympathy for the underdog. These are transformed into rancour against strangers and the elevation of individual self-interest, while we regularly step over the bodies of the underdog, the derelict, the refugee or the victim of misfortune, covered by cardboard and rags in the doorways of abandoned shops.

This is accompanied by a fearful, even superstitious, dependency upon the market – a system that lavishes its rewards and withdraws its favours in ways not amenable to distributive justice, so that human beings, once the playthings of the gods, are now at the mercy of equally capricious and unanswerable markets. Not for the first time, humanity is in thrall to its own creation.

Being there: a sense of place

To appreciate how the reimposition of these market doctrines affects flesh and blood, there is nothing like being in the places where such experiments are being carried out, sites remote from the experience of those who have conceived them.

The great epic of industrialism and its aftermath has bitten deeply into the landscape of the West Midlands. There are rough rural traces where metal workshops, forges, factories and pits have scarred the countryside. Big cities and small manufacturing settlements are separated from each other by areas of heath, canals, marsh and woodland, so that the seasons can still be read in these wild spaces – in spring, gorse and blackthorn; in summer, elder, dog-rose and willow-herb; in autumn, pale Michaelmas daisies, golden rod, bunches of black elder fruit and red hips and haws; and in winter the red stalks of cornus, dry sedge and the silvery seed-pods of traveller's joy. The local people also retain long memories of a vanished country way of life, while still enjoying fishing or bird-watching (some years ago a bird-lover in Bilston explained to me that 'In August the goldfinches feed on sugar-babbies [thistle seeds] as they blow over the railway sidings. Then they'll go onto the hard-heads [rose hips]; then when they're coming into condition for breeding, they'll feed off the dandelions in spring. That's when they come into full colour'). Industrial workers kept ferrets for catching rabbits, poached game, raced pigeons and cultivated allotments; all of which co-existed with industrial activity, fatefully lodging metal dust under the skin and in the lungs, leaving a permanent taste of metal on the tongue; or spreading coal dust, which also entered the bodies of pit-workers, alongside the feral smell of leather, or the iron savour of factories making locks, bolts, screws, rivets, chains, anchors and naval equipment – no wonder the people of the Black Country ('black by day' from smoke pollution; 'red by night' from furnaces in which the fires never went out) were regarded as a people apart. They were described by fastidious Victorian observers as 'savages', 'coarse' and 'foul-mouthed'; but theirs was an heroic labour of extraction, manufacture and creativity, without which the imperial pretensions of Britain would have been impossible.

The cities later expressed a defensive pride in their rough industrial function through civic buildings, ornate town halls with foundation stones laid by some European connection of Queen Victoria, libraries and art galleries, market halls with wrought-iron metal and stained glass, parades of shops, as well as soaring church spires and chapels designed to convert a population they never quite captured, since even when new they were rarely half full. Many of these structures still stand, in stranded and shabby splendour, too grand for the shrunken purposes of de-industrialised towns and cities; in livid stone or terracotta, with cupolas and carvings of sheaves of corn and hammers and shovels, representing agriculture and industry. Wolverhampton Art Gallery, designed to show the world a different face of the city from that associated with manufacturing, is a repository of the Victorian sensibility, containing sumptuous story-telling pictures such as *Widowed and Fatherless*, *The Harvesters* and *The Pet Bird*, and reminding the citizenry of a world beyond factories and forges in paintings of Dante and Beatrice and the ruins of Rome, scenes from Spain, Egypt, China and the Chunar Gur Fortress near Benares…

Alongside the exuberant nineteenth-century city architecture, other structures and monuments testifying to later municipal improvement have also become archaic – among them the 1930s Wolverhampton Civic Hall and the nearby plaque to Emma Sproson, 'Red Emma', the first female councillor in the city, and a feminist and socialist. Meanwhile the 1980s brutalist sprawl of council offices has been increasingly deprived of its purpose by centralising governments, as 'the provinces' have been transformed from distinctive localities into mere suburbs of globalism. In the city's Queen Square, the equestrian statue of Prince Albert – unveiled by the grieving Queen Victoria in her first public appearance outside London after his death – is no longer recognised by a new generation, for whom he is just 'the man on the horse'.

Alongside the railway lines and canals, and in the town centres, there are decaying warehouses, mills and pubs, soot still clinging to their red brick, the wasting lattice of their roofs admitting fugitive sunlight into dank mossy areas that scarcely saw daylight for a century. Ring roads have carved their scrawl into the urban fabric, making islands of town centres; motorways stride across the countryside like concrete centipedes, in the shadow of which silver-painted graffiti shows who now lays claim to these abandoned territories.

Reminders of a pre-industrial past also survive: in Wolverhampton's Queen Street, the elegant eighteenth-century County Court is up for sale. This fine building evokes the wretched who passed through its imposing doors, those tried for poaching (caught, perhaps, in the man-traps that were also manufactured in Wednesfield, from where they found their way into the parks and woods of landowners, or to slave plantations in the Caribbean), brawling, horse-stealing or the theft of a silver snuff-box from an employer, and who duly received their disproportionate deserts. The new court building is a menacing bulk, a grey fortress redolent of a different kind of wrongdoing: knife-crime, drug-dealing, grievous bodily harm. The two structures mock each other – the pillars of the eighteenth-century palace of justice meted out savage punishments for minor crimes; while the relative leniency of the dispensers of justice in the ugly contemporary structure is evidence of the altered sensibility of our time.

The workers of early industrialism are long gone, while into the diminishing red-brick terraces thrown up to serve the workshops and factories another population came – people from the Caribbean and South Asia, invited to take on jobs in the twilight industries, and to service transport and the health service. Their children and grandchildren now occupy what were originally the raw settlements of industry; inward-looking, self-protecting communities whose values of neighbourhood, family and cultural solidarity rouse ironic echoes of the people now vanished from the streets.

In the city, memory mingles with the present, as people recount their lives to one another: it seems experience is not subjective or private at all, but part of a collective pool of common understanding to be shared rather than hoarded – at the bus-stop, in the pub, on a park bench, even in strictly contemporary establishments like Greggs or Costa Coffee. After 9.30 a.m., the bus into the city centre is full of older people whose passes are valid after the rush-hour. A casual conversation, an observation overheard, provide unprompted insights into ordinary lives. A woman on the bus, perhaps in her late fifties, spontaneously starts talking about the bedroom tax. Her hand grips the metal bar of the seat in front of her; the sun strikes the wrinkles on a hand into which the wedding ring has become embedded in flesh. Without preamble, she says 'It's only a small flat. My mother died in that room. I feel I'm paying rent for her spirit.'

In an old-fashioned pub, a bleak drinking place untouched by the social amenities now associated with alcohol, a man of about 30 holds an audience of older men. 'I really fancied her. She kept looking at me, and in the end she came over and said "I'd like to have your babies." I said "OK, I'll go and fetch 'em for you. They're staying with their nan since their mam done a runner."'

A heavy-faced woman sits down with her Lidl shopping bags on a metal seat in the city centre. It is a warm summer afternoon, and her face is flushed. Warm enough for you? She is her brother's carer, and tells how she has observed his painful descent into dementia; a story familiar now in a society in which remembering was once crucial to surviving poverty and exploitation. As she spoke, I wondered whether there is some hidden connection between individual forgetting and the erasure of an industrial past which we could not quickly enough put behind us? She sheds a few tears and offers me a strong mint. Her brother's short-term memory started to go when his wife died, and he still sometimes asks where she is. For his sister, unmarried, it was natural that she should take him to live with her. Although the neighbours are kind, she dreads the coming of winter, when the curtains are drawn and *the loneliness of being together* overwhelms her. The television plays all the time; distraction and irritant. Although under pressure to work, she cannot leave her brother, who no longer recognises the streets in which he spent all his working life as a roofer. She nursed their parents until they died and then spent a few years working in a shop – 'the happiest time of my life' – until she stepped back into the shadow of caring. Sometimes angry with her brother, she weeps with remorse at the harsh words she utters. She has one friend, who will look after him if she wants to go out; but since this friend is her only source of comfort, where would she go on her own?

'My neighbour went into respite care. Her son told her it was just for a few weeks. While she was there, he sold the house, so there was nowhere for her to go back to.'

Onto the ornate Victorian exuberance a new city has been grafted; geometrical, less ornamental – colleges, hospitals, apartments, rectangles, cubes, squares. These physical changes are reflected in social attitudes, although there is a time-lag between them, so that entrenched attitudes remain. Just as two cities co-exist, so, too, do conflicting values, especially towards gender and race. Whenever I spoke to older people about their children, they would tell me their son was a mechanic, a truck driver or a shop worker, while their daughter was married and lived in Birmingham or Derby. It was always the man's work that was mentioned and the woman's status – a folk-memory which no longer applies in the modern world, where women have often become the principal earner.

The relative social peace in the cities has been assured partly by the separation of lives led by people of different cultures and ethnicities; lives intersecting only functionally – in shops, in the health service, on public transport and more substantially only in ethnically mixed neighbourhoods. A man from Jamaica who worked as a psychiatric nurse says 'Racism has gone underground since it became unlawful. In psychiatric hospitals, people do not cover up their feelings. A woman needed to be cleaned up because she had soiled herself; she said to me "Get away from me, no black man is ever going to see my bum."'

In the monumental Methodist chapel, where a foundation stone announces the worthy who laid it in the 1890s to the Glory of God, meals are offered to the hungry. Cornelius is in his forties. 'Last night I slept in the toilets in West Park. The night before that in the Bilston toilets. My cousin is disabled and in a wheelchair, and he has the keys to the public toilets. He lent them to me so I have somewhere to sleep.' He pulls aside his jacket and a set of keys, carefully labelled, hangs round his neck. 'I sleep in the baby-changing place – my feet reach the hand-dryer which is warm. I had a debt of £500 to the Council for a flat they said I had not handed the keys in for, and that has followed me for 26 years. I used to work in Quicksilver, I was called in whenever the manager dipped his hands in the till, which happened quite often. I can't work now, and there's too many CCTV cameras everywhere for a life of crime. My father is from Jamaica and my mother is on her fourth husband somewhere.'

An elderly woman with wispy white hair, sun shining against it so that it forms a silvery aureole behind her, says 'I buried my husband yesterday.' I say how sorry I am. Her weepy eyes are palest blue. A neighbour, overhearing, whispers. 'No she didn't. He died years ago.'

In St Peter's Church, an elderly Muslim sits in a pew, reading through some Christian booklets for children. His family, originally Hindu from Gujarat, came by way of Kenya to Britain. He converted when he learned that Islam supersedes all the religions that went before, and represents the last and definitive word of God. All the stories of the Jews and Christians, he says, lead up to the moment when Mohammad (PBUH) revealed truth to the world.

A café in a shopping centre: spindly chairs and tables, watery hot chocolate and weak coffee; the space echoes with children's cries, chatter and a shuffling of feet. A young woman, with two children and a Pakistani man of about 40, looks defiantly at two older women. 'I know why they're staring.' I smile at her, and she says to me 'I know what they're thinking. You can see it in their face. I was 15 when I met him, and he is the love of my life.' The man looks embarrassed. I say a few words in Urdu: he knows even less than I do. He tells me he is a van driver, and although his family resisted his marriage, they have come to respect his wife. At intervals during a busy day, people's lives open up to a moment of tenderness or vulnerability; the young woman wipes a tear at the compliment from her partner.

A woman sits in the churchyard on a bench overlooking a bed of blazing red geraniums. Here sister died recently. 'We had to wait nearly three weeks before the funeral. It's the Muslims. They have to be buried on the same day, so we have to wait. Even in death they get all the advantages.' It later turned out her sister's funeral had been at the Crematorium. I point out that Muslims have to be buried, so they couldn't have taken priority at the Crematorium. She said 'You don't understand' and walked away.

In the areas occupied now by no-longer-recent migrants and their descendants, archaic attitudes linger, ghosts of not-quite-extinct cultures. In a household of Pakistani heritage, we sit in a front room like a modernised version of an old working-class 'parlour': the outsize three-piece suite is covered with shiny plastic, so you are constantly at risk of sliding onto the floor; a plasma TV screen the focus of attention formerly occupied by a coal-fire; a cabinet full of china, trinkets and ornaments. The woman says 'They have two disabled girls next door.' 'Oh that's sad.' 'It's worse than sad', says the man. 'The husband tried to make her have an abortion because the babies were girls. Twice.'

Among men – not all of them older – from the Indian sub-continent, there is a dark murmur of resentment at what they see as the 'excessive' independence of women. 'They no longer listen to their guardians and husbands. They have picked up all these ideas about freedom, which is against our beliefs and our culture.'

These fallen patriarchs look apprehensively upon the rise of a new generation of women with careers as social workers or teachers, and are silenced by assertive observant young Muslim women – the passionate teenager, arguing against her parents in favour of the veil, who asks 'Have you never heard of the difference between bare-faced lies and veiled truths?'

In the public spaces where people's lives cross, moments of shared laughter are followed by melancholy reflection. Two young women sit at a table in the sunshine outside a café. One leans forward and says to the other 'He rolled up a tea-towel tight and stuck it in his pants. ... When he kissed her, she went to squeeze it and it was soft.' At another table, a woman talks of a friend who went on holiday to Malaga. 'They went out for a few drinks, and when they got back to the hotel, she felt thirsty, so she drank the carafe of water beside the bed. Only it wasn't water. It was the cleaning fluid they used to clean the container, which had been left in the carafe. Her brain swelled up and it killed her.'

Another sensibility lies beneath the daily business of work, child-raising, shopping and entertainment; a sense of the poignancy of life, the inseparability of its absurdity and its pleasures. In these post-industrial places, where people have lived through bewildering change, there runs a feeling of the arbitrary nature of things, the mutability of life; and with it, a far from extinct sense of solidarity, a realisation that misfortune can happen to anyone, that we shall all in our turn need the compassion and consideration of others. These values were borne by the welfare state, embodied in its agencies and institutions. They may have become hardened, no longer experienced with the vital urgency of an earlier, more insecure time. They have become dormant, waiting to be reasserted and reclaimed from their slumber in the private life of a competitive individualism. A political movement that can get beneath the skin of the clichés that float on the surface of political discourse remains tantalisingly just beyond reach. If politics leaves people cold, this is because none of it engages with a deeper humanity. There are currents of feeling in these communities, subterranean sentiments more profound than the banalities of official rhetoric, advertising slogans and received ideas. Laying hold of these deeper emotions is difficult for a political party of labour, which only two generations ago was attuned to a deep awareness of our shared destiny, our mortality and our need for the solidarity of strangers in a dangerous world – an awareness which the hucksters of this age have still not managed to dispel, despite the formidable means at their disposal for communicating the sour misanthropy of their view of the world.

The fall of industrial male labour

In the assault on the welfare system, certain groups have been disproportionately affected: women, the young, people with disability, ethnic minorities, single parents. But there is little to be gained from establishing hierarchies of suffering: despite the social shifts that have occurred with the dissolution of Britain's manufacturing base, older working men and women still bear the physical and psychological stigmata of an industrial age that has passed away.

It was upon the epic of male industrial labour, and women's unchosen subordination to it, that the wealth and power of Britain depended. Men formed for, and within, a culture of labour now effaced have received little sympathy in the recent past. But if we want to understand what has made possible the erosion of the welfare state, it is also necessary to consider the fate of older men, the descendants of those drawn into involuntary industrial servitude in the early stages of the manufacturing industry. They have been just as unceremoniously evicted from that industry in our time. Their consent was never sought, neither in the establishment of the industrial system nor in its abolition. All the momentous changes in our lives – from the nature of livelihoods to the waging of war – have been imposed by powerful others, by-passing anything remotely resembling democratic assent; and this remains constant through time.

Ken Fielden is a small wiry man in his early sixties, with a sharp mind and an intelligence that would have earned him a university education had he been born one generation later. He is at the end of a tradition of working-class intellectuals, who did much to form – and transform – the understanding of their peers in the grim workplaces of the West Midlands. He understood the implications of Margaret Thatcher's sombre prophecy 35 years ago, when she said 'Economics are the method; the object is to change the heart and soul.' The transformation of an industrial into a service economy meant not only the brick-by-brick dismantling of manufacturing, but an equally systematic unmaking and restructuring of the sensibility of the people, the long-term effects of which are only now visible, and which make possible the present assault upon welfare.

Ken started work at 15 as an apprentice tool-setter. His father told him 'You need a trade behind you.' This was seen as a guarantee of security and permanent employment, and Ken faithfully followed his father's advice. It was a tragedy that this counsel of love was negated by experience. They spoke from their own knowledge of the world, but it was a world already dissolving; the city was losing its reasons for being: tool-making, engineering, pipe-making, japanning and tinware, metal and steel jewellery and ironwork for coaches. Ken recognises the poignancy of a wisdom transmitted across the generations that society would soon annul.

The towns and cities of the West Midlands now give the impression of shrunken places. Many nineteenth-century buildings have a by-passed grandeur; spaces once occupied by streets, small workshops and factories are now car parks or wasteland; some shopping streets are almost derelict, dust clouding the windows of places where women in snoods once shaped squares of butter, or respectful assistants asked which side a gentleman dressed; pubs are boarded up where people on Saturday nights tipsily sang Danny Boy or the Rose of Tralee... Amusement arcades, betting shops, Poundland outlets, kebab houses, nail bars and tattoo salons open up in abandoned stores, bringing aspects of contemporary life to no longer vibrant thoroughfares. Everything suggests social subsidence, the dereliction of a loss of function and purpose.

Ken still bears the scars of an industrial past, although society has demolished forge and factory, and greened the sites of misery with stands of mountain ash and silver birch. The louring landscapes of work may have gone, but the injuries they inflicted remain: a good reason why efforts to demolish the elements of social welfare may be premature.

'There were nine in the family. Mother had enough to do at home without working, so it was down to Dad to support us all. I started at a power-press, tool-setting, big machines from five to fifty tons. Forklift trucks didn't exist: you had to wind up the trucks to raise and lower the load. There was no health and safety provision.' Ken holds up his right hand. The ring finger is missing and the hand is scarred. 'I was 16. Conditions were dangerous – the floor covered with dirt and metal shavings and waste that had been trodden in. There were no guards on the power-presses.

'It's funny, I never felt it. I was putting a tool onto a tool-rack, about 3 feet by 18 inches. It was very heavy. I and another man were transferring the tool to a truck, and it tilted back. I said "Tip it out" but he must have mis-heard me. My hand was trapped underneath. I felt nothing. I went to rub my hand on my chest and saw it was all red, smeared with blood. The finger was hanging off and there was a deep cut across the base of the others. My mate panicked more than I did.'

Ken worked almost 40 years tool-setting. 'I enjoyed it, but now it is a disappearing art, mostly automated. Workers are still needed to service the machines, but not in the numbers they used to. Young people have never seen a factory. Everything they buy, they don't know where it comes from, how it's made or how it got there. There is a lack of curiosity. We at least asked questions.'

A culture of want echoes in the conversation of older workers like Ken: 'I was brought up with the adage that if you don't work, you don't eat. We understood the value of money, not for money's sake, but because we valued the labour that earned it. It was thanks to the skills we had acquired that we could maintain ourselves and the people we loved.

'I grew up in a council house. It was my father's pride that he always put enough grub on the table. When I started work, who could have predicted how I would finish? I am an apprentice care assistant in a residential care-home for the elderly, 40 one-bedroom flats in the complex. I have done eight months on an apprentice wage of £2.68 an hour. After a year, I'll go on to the minimum wage. When I was an apprentice in the metal trade, it meant something. Now it's an insult. My age and experience count for nothing. After tool-setting for 35 to 40 years, I'm working 35 hours a week for less than a hundred pounds. It's not a question of work, it's about dignity.

'I did other jobs in between. You could walk in and out of work as you pleased then. I did metal-polishing, whisky flasks. Two years, the dust got everywhere, even wearing a mask, you could taste the metal. Then I worked in a saddlery, making the girths that held the saddle on. I did hand- and machine-stitching, leather preparing. Once you have learned to use your hands, you can turn them to anything. I have been out of work in my life precisely 18 months. Then I was offered this apprentice scheme. I love working with people, but the idea that I have to be trained to do it is humiliating. I looked after my own parents. It's come to something when people have to be taught how to care.

'My father was impaired as a result of his occupation. He was also in engineering. His job was to lift loads manually and place them on the floor. Bending continuously wore his hip away. He had a metal plate inserted in his late forties and after that, couldn't work again.

'My mother also lost a leg in later life. An ingrowing toenail was not treated and became infected. She had a toe off, then two, then all her toes and then her foot. In the end, they took the leg off at the knee – bit by bit the infection had spread and they hadn't cut it all out.

'Of the nine children, one brother died at two and a half in 1960; another died two years ago. He had chest pains and went to the hospital. They told him it was indigestion. He walked out of the hospital, went home and died.

'When I first started work, I gave all my money to my mother. You tipped up your wages and she gave you spending money. When our parents died, the family became less close. The bonds weakened. But while I worked in industry, our mates were our brothers. We looked after one another, because the work was dangerous, and we were always in jeopardy.

'I'm lucky. I have plenty of inner resources. I'm poor now, the money is crap, but I'm helping people less fortunate than myself. When they smile and thank you, that is part of the reward. I was the first in my family to learn a trade. Before that, they had been just labourers. I have always striven to better myself, not just financially, but morally, intellectually. I can do better today than I did yesterday. I've used my intelligence to improve myself and other people. That gives you a fulfilment different from money.

'When I look at the young, I feel a mixture of compassion and anger. They have no sense of social purpose. The working class has changed: it seems they don't give a damn for others. It isn't their fault – they are created by social values, they don't determine those values. We had to strive for the things we wanted: young people seem to think if we sit here long enough, everything will come to us.

'I get paid monthly, £378.31. I have some savings, which I am dipping into because I need the car for work. Tax and MOT are coming up. Our standard of living has suffered. All the clothes I'm wearing, apart from my trousers, are second-hand. We don't buy branded or named products any more. We live on basics. I do without things I used to love: liver – I never eat liver now. It seems a small thing, but you miss it. If we buy ham, we buy it in a plastic packet. That's £2. If you were to buy it fresh cooked from the butcher's, you'd get only four slices for the same price.

'As a care assistant, I am responsible for personal care, bathing, medication. Your aim is to promote maximum independence. When I hear about the abuse of old people in care homes, it makes me sick to the stomach. I also hate the way they refer to people in the homes as "customers". Customers are people who go into shops. It turns people into a commodity. I've always taken it for granted that we care for one another. It came naturally to us. Caring is priceless. Perhaps that's why it's considered worthless – in this society, there is no such thing as beyond price.

'When I look at this town, metals and making stuff is virtually extinct; and so are we, the people who worked with them.'

Ken has done what many men evicted from heavy industry have not: he has remained to face what he sees as the degradation of labour. He has not run away. He is part of the majority of people who, however poor, are not idle, but always ache to be doing something constructive and useful. Even on the dole, he did voluntary work. He takes his membership of the working class with unfashionable seriousness: 'That's what I do. I have to be working. I feel sorry for anyone who wants to sit on their backside doing nothing. It makes their lives pointless.' Ken sees idleness as a pathology; as though 'doing nothing' were everyone's dream, and only 'shirkers' get away with it. It isn't only a Puritanical heritage that speaks through him, but a sense that our passage through time needs to be marked by durable, creative labour. He is angry, both at a society that has given up the making of useful and necessary things, and at the people who have let such purposes slip away without protest. He views with distaste those men who have run away from their communities.

'Running away' does not necessarily mean absconding. Significant numbers of men have fled the post-industrial environment by disengaging from responsibility for family, children, livelihood. Even in the industrial age, there were many who spent most of their money on drink or gambling. But theirs was an escape within the community: it used to be said of almost every industrial town in Britain that the shortest way out of it was through the pub door.

Today a generation of wandering men are fugitives from society. They do not live with partners, families or children, and often evade their obligations in making payments to them. Many women have given up expecting maintenance for children from those who have disappeared, concealing themselves in the anonymity of male rootlessness. Women remain, as women do everywhere in the world.

I met two men who were unsure of how many children they had fathered. They had worked, but were retired, both with a disability. They did not express feelings of guilt or regret that they were never involved in permanent relationships or in their children's upbringing. The ruins of industry also left another form of wreckage, a disinheritance of humanity, among people who took flight from derelict industrial neighbourhoods, seeking refuge in the fantasies offered by capitalism: a wandering life of temporary lodgings, casual work and random relationships, a reach-me-down culture of 'moving on', of restless curiosity about the world, almost a celebration of detachment from place and purpose. Some young men who have left their families talk about 'finding themselves', 'taking off', even 'seeing the world', when that world is often only another town that used to make ceramics, steel or boots. The removal of the economic base of these places casts a long shadow over the generations that follow, a dissatisfaction of the spirit, an unbelonging. Many such towns had scarcely recovered from the violence in which they had been conceived before they had to adapt to the sweeping away of the harsh culture of labour; and however great the advantages of change, a scarring of the psyche remains.

That it is women – and children – who pay the price of the 'freedoms' men permit themselves goes without saying; although the ways in which they do so can be surprising and tragic. Many women I met mentioned, almost casually, the abuse they had suffered from fathers, uncles, brothers, husbands or sons. In poor communities – unleavened by the educated and informed – conservative social attitudes can still be found; a last resting-place, as it were, of values and beliefs that were, until the very recent past, social norms. Racism, bigotry and sexism find a receptive shelter in the hearts of some of the most disadvantaged.

Poverty, it seems, can be a great social conserver, an embalmer of archaic attitudes and sentiments officially abandoned. The poor occupy not only the most polluted parts of cities, but also a kind of toxic dump for ideas which dominated society until quite recently: they wear ideological shreds and patches discarded by elites, just as they haunt reach-me-down charity and thrift shops, snapping up the leftovers of those whose wakeful eyes are open to the necessities of the hour.

Benefit fraud

Andy, in his fifties, was done for benefit fraud in 2001: he had worked while still signing on as unemployed. He had been told by the then newly formed Department for Work and Pensions that he was allowed to work up to 16 hours a week, without loss of benefits. He took this to mean that he would lose no benefits, provided he worked no longer than those hours.

Andy does not read or write. He could make no sense of letters and documents which came through the post. He had no idea he was doing anything wrong and made no effort at concealment. He received a court summons in 2001, and was shocked to learn that the Department claimed he owed them thousands of pounds. He has been paying back £7.20 a week for 13 years. In 2015, he was told the rate of payment will be increased to £28.25 a week. At this level of repayment, the debt will be cleared by 2024. What kind of a life is it, he asks, to have to spend a quarter of a century in debt for an error?

Andy had hidden nothing. He is, he says, guilty of ignorance, and is the first to admit that not being literate is a serious social handicap – indeed it led to his present circumstances.

'I thought nothing of it. My friend, Rose, was working with a woman who had been sacked, and her cleaning job was going. I took it. I just worked. Other cleaning contracts came in. I made sure I never went over 15 hours, so I thought everything was in order. It lasted five years. I would do a number of jobs a day – half an hour here, an hour there – in the Chamber of Commerce, night clubs, the rugby club, banks, even the Magistrates' Court. I didn't understand the forms I was sent. I should have got help, but it seemed simple and straightforward. It was a friend – ex-friend – who got jealous of me and grassed me up. He has moved to North Wales; otherwise I would have punched his head in.

'My solicitor explained my situation to the Court. I got twelve months' probation, and an order to pay back the sum I had claimed. I was also sent on a reading and writing course at the Probation Office. It lasted four days because I was the only one who turned up. The alternative to paying back the money was three years in prison – it was mostly Jobseeker's Allowance and Disability Living Allowance.

'The Department agreed to the low rate at which I could pay. The Debt Management team had to prove hardship – medical expenses and so on – and £7.20 was agreed on. I am not appealing against the rise, although my budget is so tight I have barely enough to live on.'

As dusk falls, the room grows dark. Andy does not usually put the lights on. This saves a small amount each week. Because he has visitors, he turns on the single 60-watt bulb. There is no shade, since that would diminish the already meagre light. The room is sparingly furnished: a big sofa, two armchairs. Andy's is a battered but comfortable chair which rocks and swivels. A small mat covers a patch of the bare floorboards. The only other items are a television and a table. It is a cheerless place, but that does not trouble Andy, since he likes to be out of doors. He never feels cold and does not use heating even in the coldest weather.

As in most houses I visited, the chill is numbing. It was January. Perpetual cold is accepted as a natural condition by many poor people. In other houses, a single radiator, an electric fire with a single bar on a curved metal panel, or a halogen heater, tempered the worst of it. People sat muffled in blankets, sweaters and eiderdowns; inhabitants of another climate, social if not meteorological.

Andy is a keen fisherman. 'The best things in life don't cost anything. I love fishing. The canal has carp, pike, tench and bream. I went there a couple of weeks ago and the police were out in force, checking everybody and their gear. Some Iranians have been camping along the canal: carp is their national fish, and they had been taking them for eating. We only fish for the sport. I never eat anything I catch.

'I lost my parents when I was five. They died within a few months of each other. My mother had a burst ulcer and my father a heart attack. He was a long-distance lorry driver. I hardly knew what had happened. I was sent to my nan's sister who had a farm in Yorkshire. I roamed the countryside, which I loved. I was driving a tractor at the age of eight or nine. My nan and aunties looked after me.

'As a kid, I was disruptive. My own life had been disturbed, and that must have made me wild. At that time, a child's feelings were not considered. They packed you off wherever they thought you'd be safe. They looked after me, but that was as far as it went. I came back to Wolverhampton at 15. I went into lodgings. I got tangled up with my sister's husband, who was a bit rough; he led me astray, you might say. At 15, 16 we were pinching blue lights off the top of police cars and selling them to travellers.

'I was done for fighting a copper. I beat him up and broke his jaw. I had to go to Court on my birthday, 1976. I was sentenced to three years in prison, Winson Green in Birmingham, and from there to Wormwood Scrubs. On appeal the sentence was reduced to one year in a young offenders' prison and then Borstal. After that, I swore I would never go inside again. I had also been done for drinking and driving, then for driving while I was disqualified. I was a tearaway.

'But I worked. You could leave a job dinner time and start a new one the same afternoon. The first one I went for, I told them I couldn't read or write. They said "That's OK, start Monday." It didn't matter. I worked in a plastic-mould-ing foundry, making frames for television sets and hi-fis. Then I went on to welding. The factory backed on to the canal. I cleared a space behind the factory, so I could fish. I went night-fishing, all over – Berkswell, Hampton-in-Arden, Stourbridge. I love fishing. We always go out first time in the season on my birthday – April 23rd. Rose brings her magazines and we sit in the sunshine.

'I got married in 1983. It lasted 15 years. It was all right until I came home from work early one night and found her in bed with my best friend. I lost my wife and best mate all in one day. Our two daughters went with her after the divorce. I don't know where they are. I haven't seen the oldest since she was nine. She'd be 22 now; somebody told me she had been looking for me at my old address.

'I never had the patience to learn to read and write. I liked to be outside. I couldn't settle in school or concentrate. I have suffered from depression. I still do. But I've always done voluntary work. Three days a week I go to Coventry. I repair old cycles, a workshop in a church building. We get bikes rusty, buckled wheels, smashed up. I rebuild them, spray and refurbish them so they can be sold.

'When I got severe depression I would lock myself away for days on end. I would go into my room and just not come out. I was sent to a psychiatrist, but all he gave me was tablets.

'I'm getting £195 a fortnight benefit, Employment and Support Allowance, and £80 Disability Living Allowance. I get a bit extra, because of my commitment to voluntary work. If things are a lot better now, it's because of Rose.'

Rose, a woman in her fifties, has, she says, 'sorted him out'. They are close neighbours. Rose's husband suffers from Alzheimer's. Andy and Rose share the caring of him. Rose says 'I met Andy in the drop-in centre after he had his breakdown. He moved in with my husband and me for a few months.' Andy says 'Until I met Rose, I used to throw bills in the bin. I was evicted and had nowhere to go. She was the saving of me.'

Andy has a lasting feud with the energy company, Npower, over his utility bills. Originally, he was to have occupied a different flat in the block, and his bills were sent there. He never received them. The company tried to charge him for finding his whereabouts when it did locate him, although it had been given the correct address at the beginning. He was charged for electricity and gas he never used in a flat he never occupied. 'They can only charge twelve months in arrears, so the rest was cancelled.' It was the fault of the company, which is now not prepared to accept the £40 a month he is paying on the accumulated bills in his present flat. 'I economise. I only turn on the hot water on Sunday, when I have a shower. If you're cold, you have to wrap yourself up in a duvet.'

Andy does not eat breakfast. In the middle of the day, he makes a sandwich or buys a bun. His main meal is a £1 frozen dinner from the market. He shows me what he will eat tonight: three or four dark slices of beef in gravy, a spoonful of carrots and peas and some slices of potato, in a plastic container with a film covering. Although neither nourishing nor sufficient, the £7 Andy spends each week on these meals is his principal food outlay. He never eats fruit, but has several cups of tea each day, which quell the pangs of hunger.

Empty fridges purring away, using up electricity on nothing to keep cool; bare containers, out-of-date milk curdled in a plastic bottle, unappetising ready-made tagliatelle, pot-noodles, a bag of rice, sliced bread in a plastic wrapper – these are the material indices of contemporary poverty, with its attendant malnutrition: perpetual colds, successive infections, costs uncounted in cut and 'sanctioned' benefits, and simply passed on to the health service or other agencies that pick up the casualties of this *contrived deprivation*. Immune-systems depressed, resistance lowered by what is called 'self-neglect', even though it is not self-inflicted at all.

Just as Rose has been a support to Andy, he in turn helps her deal with her husband's Alzheimer's. They are taking him into town today to get some new trousers: he has lost a lot of weight, and cannot find his own way around the town he has known all his life. Rose and her husband have six children: one in Mexico, another in New Zealand. One boy is gay and lives with his partner in Shropshire, where they run a hotel. Rose has one handicapped daughter, who is a twin. 'She is not very badly affected, but there was a slight injury to her brain at birth. I see her a lot. I am close to her.'

Sometimes, it is a glaringly obvious – but apparently disregarded – element that keeps people poor. Andy's double bereavement at the age of five in the 1960s was not considered sufficiently important for anyone to consider its influence on his emotional development. He was 'looked after', but that did not mean he was cared for. No one gave him any explanation, let alone compensatory affection, on the death of his parents. His inability to concentrate, his 'wild' youth, his failure to acquire the basic skills of reading and writing – how much of this could have been remedied, had he come into contact with people with insight into the needs of children damaged so early by loss? This lack of recognition of bereavement or disturbance in children pursues many people for a lifetime, and contributes to their poverty.

Childhood trauma has been acknowledged in the effects on children of sexual abuse, but sympathy for other forms of violence, emotional abuse and lovelessness is largely absent, even though such experiences are no less damaging. We may wonder why recognition of sexual abuse is the only aspect of violence against children that has stirred the conscience of adults in recent years. Is it because we feel guilty at the over-sexualisation of society? Why can't the harm wrought by emotional and psychological trauma be subject to the same searching inquiry? Many adults are haunted by the brutality, indifference or casual cruelty which have inhibited their capacity to compete with the self-assured and confident (and often, self-righteous). It would not do to investigate such roots of poverty, especially in those whose plight is ascribed by government and its ideological allies to moral failings, in order to gain acceptance for the castigation it inflicts upon the 'undeserving'. A more generous understanding of human frailties would interfere with these simple categories and is therefore avoided.

Of course, many people do overcome the most severe disadvantages; but a disproportionate number do not, and it is they who are on the receiving end of public disapproval, moral censure and punitive government policy.

A fate foretold

Although misfortune can force anyone onto the wasting charity of the welfare state, it is obvious that many whose long-term needs have created what the government calls 'a culture of dependency' have suffered in their lives, often in childhood. I do not know of studies that track the life-experience of those more or less continuously on benefit. Such investigations might reveal the early losses or experiences of violence that prevent some adults from developing the qualities required for steady and regular employment. They might reveal how their youthful abilities were undermined by distress which inhibited them from achieving what might have been within their grasp.

Any such deeper interrogation of people's lives would reveal the shallowness of social cant about 'level playing fields', 'equality of access', 'fulfilling their potential', and all the other staples of vacuous political rhetoric. Rather than curbing 'welfare', it would be more humane – not to mention more economically efficient (and this might appeal to the votaries of the 'bottom line') – to establish a more flexible and more merciful approach to 'claimants', a word become pejorative, and more usually associated with a gold rush or a disputed will.

It doesn't require psychoanalysis to sympathise with *Mary*, now in her late forties, who was adopted soon after her 15-year-old mother gave birth. She and a boy two years older were taken in by a devout Anglican family who had no children. Within three years of the adoption, the family had a child of their own, a little girl. Mary says 'It was obvious from the start that we were second-class children; and I was even more second-class because I was only a girl. They even changed my name. I was called Pearl, but they changed it to Mary. Our sister – she was no relation – was a princess, and we were her servants. We were objects of charity, treated differently – bathed once a week in a few inches of bath water with a mixture of washing-up liquid and disinfectant. This was an attempt by our foster parents to wash away the stains of our polluted origins. And that wasn't all. They cut us off from our real families. They wanted to make sure that their wicked ways would have no influence on us, and we would become as godly and virtuous as they were. When I asked about my birth mother, they said she was no good, and didn't want me. I later found out my mother regretted all her life having given me up.

'I hated the church and I don't remember a time when I believed in it. I was a misfit. I felt it more than my brother, because as a boy he had more freedom. They had to watch over me, the daughter of a fallen woman. How could a girl of 15 be a prostitute, because that was the word my foster mother once used of her. I was angry, always angry. I was a trouble-maker at school – the stigma followed me. I was always being suspended, and when I got home I'd be punished. That was nothing new, because I was always being punished just for living. They didn't beat me. They locked me in the bedroom for hours on end and made me eat things I hated, spinach and sprouts, and until I ate it, I wouldn't be given anything else.

'My adoptive father worked in the City Treasurer's department. He shared this rigid view of the world. I married at 17. He was an electrician, 25. My parents refused to come to the wedding, because it was in the registry office and I didn't want anything to do with the church. The marriage didn't last. I felt I wasn't good enough for him, and he must have thought I was right because he found someone else.

'I taught myself a lot, but my biggest teacher was my own experience of life; and bitter lessons it gave me. Always an outsider, I could never make friends. I am not stupid. I have read a lot. I think lonely people do. I have worked in care homes, shops, offices, cleaning. I'm not proud. But I could never get on with people – they were always ganging up against me. I have been on and off benefit, because I get periods of depression. I left one place because I was becoming paranoid. I was sanctioned for that. I couldn't explain. I shouted at them in the Jobcentre. I called them ignorant and prejudiced, which they are.'

Those who, as children, have been objects of malice, cruelty, emotional and mental violence have seen neither their concerns addressed, nor the slightest interest in the enduring effects of the humiliation and unkindness they have received. Yet many are now being punished afresh by cuts to a grudging welfare system which, far from making any attempt to heal the scars of youthful injury, now stigmatises them as shirkers, idlers or chancers.

And those who do survive the indifference of society to their suffering, often find that youthful ambition, intelligence and capacity have been undermined by emotional insecurity and a lack of self-regard or confidence; all of which adds up to a terrible squandering of human resources in a society which pleads public poverty in a world of unparalleled private affluence.

Jordan suffered similar neglect on the death of his mother.

'My mum died when I was seven. I remember seeing the ambulance come to the house in Faith Street. She was taken out on a stretcher. When they came out of the door, I ran after the ambulance and fell down. My nan picked me up and took me back into the house. We went to the hospital. I don't remember much else. We sat outside the ward. She had cancer. She did smoke 80 cigarettes a day, but she was only in her thirties.

'After she died, my father soon found a new partner, Sandra. I moved in with them, but he was more for her than for me. I reminded him of his life with my mother which made him uncomfortable. So I was passed round the family. I lived with my father's brothers and sisters, and then with my nan and granddad in London.'

Jordan had a long spell of unemployment before his present job as a gardener for a housing association. He maintains the grounds of sheltered accommodation, old people's homes and the area around blocks of flats – hedge-cutting, pruning, planting, tree-cutting and clearing dead leaves. This, of all the work he has done, is the most congenial. At 50, he realises horticulture is what he ought to have been doing all his life; only no one ever found out what he preferred. No one paid any attention to his needs or skills. To have done so when he was young was not the way of the world.

'I'm up at six, out at seven o'clock in the morning, at work by eight. The work is in hostels, housing schemes, care homes. This time of year, it's mainly cutting back and pruning. In summer, there's keeping the grass down, while picking up litter is a round-the-year job. In winter, we clean up all the sites, clear flower beds, put bark over them and turn over the soils. I love it. My biggest fear is that they might say they no longer need me. I'd have to give up this flat.'

Jordan recently separated from his partner of 22 years, with whom he remains on good terms. 'My ex-missis – I call her my missis although we never married – was always there for me. She helped me a lot in life, and I feel grateful to her. We still get on. Neither of us has found anybody else. But we were bickering all the time, and it wasn't good around the children. Gideon is now 17; there's a girl, 15, a boy 13, a boy 9 and a girl 8. We still think of ourselves as a family unit. I'm there for them. If I'm needed, they know where I am. I only have to get on my bike. I'll love her till I go to my grave.'

They had seven children together, one of whom, little Jordan, was a Down's syndrome baby. 'We lost him at ten months. That's his picture on the wall. I still miss him. He had a hole in his heart, and died of what they call "natural causes". He always had a smile on his face. The hospital said there was nothing we could have done to prevent his death.'

If Jordan identifies so keenly with the little boy who died, this is perhaps because he sees something of his own bereavement as a child in the loss in his son. Living alone has given him space to think. 'Life goes on. Before I leave this earth, I want to know that my kids are going to be all right. OK for money, a roof over their heads, happiness.'

Jordan's father died last year. Reflecting on his own life, he says he was accepted only on sufferance. At 18, he returned to Wolverhampton, and lived with his mate's family. 'Then I went into bed and breakfast. I never felt wanted. I had to bring myself up.

'After I came back here, I sometimes met my dad in the street. He would say "Hello", but never stop for a conversation. I look like my mum. He didn't want to know me. He felt guilty because he found and married Sandra before my mother had had time to rest.

'My father worked till he was 74. I wanted to see him before he died. I wanted to say my piece, and at the same time, let him know I did love him. I got his address from my uncle, his twin brother. I was putting on my shoes, ready to go and visit him in the hospital. My uncle called. "Where are you?" "I'm just going to the hospital." "I'm not being funny, but he's in the mortuary." I was told only at the last moment. I didn't want to argue with my uncle, but when I had gone to him for comfort, he pushed me away. I hadn't seen him since I was 16.

'I went to pay my respects at his funeral, not to quarrel with his family. My uncle offered me his hand. I couldn't shake it. The first time my son saw his granddad, it was on a mortuary slab. My uncle said to me 'Where have you been these 30 years?' He knew where I was. I hadn't been in hiding. It was just that he didn't want any relationship with me. I said to my son "Come on we're going."

'I feel bitter about my father dying and his brother not letting me know in time. That done my head in, not seeing him, his twin not telling me how sick he was. My father and his brother were both builders. They knocked around as a foursome when they were young, the twins and their wives. My cousin said to me "I don't think your dad wanted you." That was it. He wanted me out of the way.

'I barely went to school. I couldn't settle. And I didn't understand then what had happened to me. As a kid, I worked in a bakery, instead of going to school: I used to take the buns, baps and pikelets out of the oven. When I left school, I went on a youth employment scheme and learned painting and decorating. I worked for years in a saddlery, making frames for saddles. Then I was a labourer in a builder's yard, driving a fork-lift truck, loading and unloading wagons. After that I went to a food company, working at the back of the premises, wrapping the food in silver foil containers like in a Chinese take-away.

'I wanted the job I have now ever since I was a kid. I should have gone to work in Parks and Gardens, but there was no one to guide me, and no one thought to find out what I wanted.

'My nan and granddad gave me the most stability. He had been in the military. A grenade went off and he got shrapnel in his face. Later, he became chair-ridden and had multiple sclerosis. I looked on them as my mother and father.

'When I was small, my father used to hit me with a belt, because that was how his father used to hit him. It's all changed now. You don't treat kids like that anymore. I would never do that to mine. The only good thing my father did was teach me how to fish. I have fished in the same spot for 25 years. I used to fish near a copper works. Because of the pollution, you caught fish that were deformed or had three eyes. I once caught an eel in the canal. I told my granddad. He said he used to go sea-fishing, and had once caught some eels which he released into the canal years ago. The one I got must have been from those he put there all that time ago.'

Just as industrial accidents leave their physical traces on the injured bodies of workers, emotional damage leaves its own raw wounds and unseen injuries that work against people's ability to thrive. Jordan's separation from his partner seemed a kind of elective bereavement, an echo of the death of his mother when he was seven, playing itself out now in middle life. Warm and sociable, he nevertheless exudes an underlying melancholy. When he speaks of his life, he recognises that the psychological and social source of what troubles him began long ago, in a life shadowed by griefs unacknowledged for years.

It would be good to think we had progressed since the time when Mary and Jordan were children; yet the experiences of those who have been in care as more recent wards of the State suggest that whatever sympathy may be extended to children, it is abruptly withdrawn as soon as they become adults, even if they are haunted for a lifetime by the unhealed social and psychological lesions of class.

Sheltered accommodation

In sheltered accommodation for the elderly, many women in their eighties and nineties can still recall the old industrial environment while it was relatively intact and traditional workplaces were the major source of employment in the city. These survivors maintain a choral commentary on the fading epic of industrial life. Like those who worked in the pits, mills and forges, they led lives of poverty and insecurity, but salvaged from it a certain austere grandeur. Their rage against oppression gave dignity to their suffering, because, despite it all, they still lived with the hope of a better world. That better world was indeed established, and much of the misery they knew removed.

If the happiness that might have been expected to accompany it has failed to materialise, this is, perhaps, because that social hope which sustained earlier generations has been extinguished. Hope has been, arguably, the most dramatic privatisation of all. There is now, apparently, no better world to be struggled for. Capitalism, rather than being just one social and economic system among others, today determines the limits of the known and knowable worlds; and all discussion must take place within its confines. This has involved a collective impoverishment beyond measure. It has reduced human beings to 'economic units', and interprets lives as though the creation and spending of wealth were the sole purpose of existence. It suppresses both the splendour and tragedy of being alive and replaces the sense of a shared predicament with concern for individual destinies. It creates market dependency and bids us to regard this as the necessary condition and definition of what it means to be human.

It is much harder to resist this diminution of our lives than to confront the desolation of chronic want and hunger. We lack the vocabulary to discuss the mutations of contemporary poverty, and continue to frame our criticisms in the shadow of a past industrial society. Resistance to the version of capitalism that provides all the counterfeits – consumerism instead of prosperity, money instead of security, individualism instead of pride in the uniqueness of everyone, a contrived competitiveness in a world overflowing with abundance – is a different kind of struggle from that against squalor and want.

Of course the women remember male tyranny and rejoice at its overthrow; but it was a reflection, in the domestic sphere, of the oppressions and hierarchies of work. 'Women knew that all that stood between their children and destitution was the power of men to provide.' The men of the industrial era were also victims, and it was one of the great tragedies of the labour movement that it largely failed to intervene in those 'private' spaces where men readily meted out to captives of domesticity a version of the same violence that had been dealt them. Was it lack of imagination, or simply the urgency of survival, which made labour organisations insensitive to the world beyond the workplace, leading them to overlook the context in which people lived and hoped and dreamed? Whatever the reason, a high price has been paid by the trade unions and the labour movement for their inability to extend their concerns beyond the workplace and into the social arrangements that resulted from a division of labour which was reflected in the domestic sphere with such destructive power.

'We lived in poverty but we also lived in hope' is how the old women express it. 'When I worked everywhere used to be so dirty. I was in a leather-factory, making bridles for horses. My sister worked in a press. She lost the tops of her fingers – you hadn't to let your attention wander for a second. None of the machines had guards on them. It was just an occupational hazard. It was common to see people injured at work; you sometimes couldn't tell who was hurt in the war and who was hurt in the factories.' Emily, 83, recalls: 'There was a smell of metal: metal dust and shavings, I can still remember it clung to people's clothes, got under their nails, and of course, entered their lungs. That's why so many women are widows. … I got 18 shillings for my first week at work. I was 14. You gave all your money to your parents, and they gave you a shilling a week to spend on yourself.'

Laura, whose father was a bus driver, is proud that her father didn't take the children out of school as soon as he could so that they could earn money. 'He let us go to the grammar school. He was very enlightened. As you get older, it helps if you've had the kind of background where you want to keep in touch with the world. Reading and listening. I've been here for 18 years. In that time it has changed. There is less going on for people than there was. All activities for the residents have been cancelled by cuts. There used to be Bingo, coffee mornings, talks. Now there is nothing. We are bored.'

'I came here when I lost my husband', says Gracie, who is 79. 'I just didn't want to stay in the house where I had spent so many happy years. The memories were too painful. I mean, we had our arguments. He could be terrible when he'd had a drink. But as he got older, he quietened down. He loved his home, and I tried to make it as cheerful for him as I could.'

Zubeida

An archaic inheritance of male dominance characterises many Muslim communities. Tradition becomes stronger in the face of insecurity; values harden in a hostile environment. As if this were not enough, the benefits system has now turned its unsympathetic attention to lone Muslim women widowed or deserted, upon whom it now places pressure to find work. Women in late middle age, who have raised a family and looked forward to being maintained by them, now find themselves bereft of support and abandoned by a welfare system, which demands they enter an unfamiliar and unwelcoming labour market. Humiliated and rejected, their social role as 'home-makers' is now discounted; their expectation that, their purpose fulfilled, they would be taken care of, was an illusion.

Zubeida, a spare energetic woman in her mid forties, is smartly dressed because she has just come from yet another job search. In the past three months she has visited factories and workplaces all over Wolverhampton in a desperate bid to find work. Zubeida came to Britain 25 years ago from a village in Azad Kashmir. A bride at 16, she was married to a man she had never seen, in a country about which she had heard only distant rumours.

Zubeida was delighted I could speak some Urdu; and she responded with sad candour: 'I came with a head and a heart full of dreams. We had no land in Kashmir. I thought a new life would open to me. It did, but it was one I could never have anticipated. My husband had lived here for many years. He came as a child with his parents. For the first two months, the marriage went smoothly, but after that, he treated me cruelly.'

Zubeida, little more than a child herself, had no one to turn to. Two children were born in the seven years the marriage lasted; one is now 25, the other 18. It ended 19 years ago, when Zubeida's husband left to live with another woman. He advised her to get married again, and took no responsibility for the children.

'The only relative I had was my auntie, my mother's sister. She has been my help and support. I brought up the boys on benefit, but now they are adult, I am expected to find work. My benefits are sanctioned for three months, because they said I was not trying hard enough. I have no other source of income. I give Anwar five pounds each day to go to college. I stopped receiving benefits at the end of November, and now we are in

February. I worked once with the Fresh Sandwich Company, and during that time I got working tax credit and child tax credit, £135 a week. I have been all over the city. I hope to go on to Jobseeker's Allowance. Our rent is £55 a week, but we have arrears of over £1,200.

'I have walked every street and applied to every factory in the city.' Zubeida showed me the booklet, in which the Jobcentre expects her to enter a note of every place to which she has applied, to say how she reached the factory, and to describe the outcome. Her elder boy had completed the entries for earlier applications, and I filled in those she had just finished – food-packing jobs, plastics factories, stores from Wednesbury to West Bromwich to Smethwick. She must provide the address and telephone number, so her story can be verified. 'I find it upsetting to go to the Jobcentre. They treat you as though are stupid and make you feel you are nothing.'

It is a profoundly shaming experience for someone of her maturity and imagined status. Each attempt has to be signed off by someone called a 'Coach', who ticks a box on the page, as though she were a football trainee. A plastic folder contains her curriculum vitae, also supervised by a Jobcentre employee: a thin, sad document. Apart from packing sandwiches, there is little employment history to record. A single paragraph sums up her life: 'I have been a home-maker, and brought up my two children. I can clean, cook and look after a house.' Another paragraph explains that her 'hobbies' (!) are 'reading, watching TV and walking'. This bland information gives no idea of the struggle of a woman who has devoted her life to her children, and for whom it is her primary contribution to society. That her elder boy is also unemployed only adds to the injury of her unrecognised effort. It is one thing to castigate people for their want of striving; but it gives no credit to those who have done their utmost, putting themselves through great hardship, with little visible effect. The inability – or unwillingness – of government and the companies it employs to make such elementary distinctions is a source of much suffering and great anger.

Suddenly, Zubeida's life, with all its pain, grief and effort, is opened up for the world to see and set at small worth. The pride at having survived as a single parent in a community in which this is a source of shame is unvalued by those whose sole focus is the 'placement' of people in jobs for which they have neither the experience nor aptitude. Zubeida weeps. Tears darken her blue saree. There is, apparently, 'no market' for the valour and dignity of people, their stoicism under stress and the brave face they have assumed, when inside they feel they have failed wretchedly.

'My auntie's husband died 20 years ago, and she is now a pensioner. The £70 she contributes to the household each week has saved us. She lives with us; without her, I could not have continued. Our house is cold, since we cannot afford heating. We are four at home. My older son is married. His wife lives with her family in Azad Kashmir. He visits her there. He only came back last month, and must wait three months before he can get Jobseeker's Allowance. He was working as a waiter in Birmingham. He was with me in the sandwich factory before going to see his wife. When he was looking for work, he gave his CV at one shop, and they simply threw it into the bin in his presence.

'My boys know I have been both father and mother to them. I am the only woman in the street on her own, but I have good neighbours: on one side Bengalis, on the other, an African family. I have survived until today thanks to Allah. I say *namaz* five times a day.

'My father-in-law is a good man, but his wife never liked me. When I think, 25 years ago, I got on an aircraft for the first time, very frightened, but hoping for a new life, I wondered whether the husband my father had chosen would be good to me. When he beat me, I begged him to send me back home. He wouldn't, even though he later went back to Pakistan to find someone else. We cannot look for justice in this life, but we must endure. I went to Azad Kashmir 22 years ago, after my father's death, and then for my son's wedding. My life is here.'

Zubeida's wounded self-respect is tangible. Insulted emotionally and socially, she is treated with contempt by employees of the Jobcentre half her age. Women of her generation, enclosed in family life, did not learn English fully, since their lives were based in the domestic sphere, and everyone spoke the language of home. Expelled from that fragile security, and turned into an involuntary outcast, she is apparently no longer one of the government's beloved 'strivers', despite the efforts she has made all her life. It is against these silent struggles to retain a sense of self-esteem that a 'reformed' benefits system strikes with such violence. In July 2015, it was announced that advisers to the Department for Work and Pensions would look at the 'effectiveness' of benefits sanctions. There is apparently little evidence that they 'drive' people into work; to assess how many they drive to despair is doubtless not part of its remit.

'Sanctions' is itself a politically charged word. For sanctions are what Western governments impose upon 'outlaw' regimes – Russia, North Korea, Iran – to make them conform to the desires of an 'international community'. That the poor in

Britain should be subject to the same policy demonstrates that they are perceived by our rulers in the same way that they view other delinquent entities in the world.

Azma

Azma was also abandoned by her husband. Originally from Sialkot in Pakistan, in 2000 she, too, was left with children – three small boys, the youngest six months old. Her husband remarried, and the children lost all contact with their father.

When I met Azma, she was returning to her terraced house from the shops. Aged 45, she is partly disabled, and finds it difficult to negotiate the step into her house. She has diabetes, is arthritic and suffers from depression. In the room – illuminated by one window looking onto the yard – there are two sofas facing each other. On a side-table there are photographs of the boys, including a picture of the graduation ceremony of her eldest, who recently left Keele University with a degree in Biomedical Sciences. Unable to find work in his chosen field, he is employed in a department store. The second boy, Shafkhat, is unemployed, while the youngest – whose ambition is to teach – is still at school studying for his A levels.

Like Zubeida, Azma too had never seen the husband she came to join in Britain 23 years ago. It is impossible to overstate the shock experienced by young women, who have rarely gone far from their house, on coming to Britain, a mythic land of wealth, progress and an imperial power not quite faded from memory. They find in the West Midlands a dingy greyness, and forms of poverty they had never encountered before; once here, they face for the first time the individual and his family, with whom it is their destiny to spend a lifetime. Azma's husband left 16 years ago. She brought up the children on benefit, and no one disturbed her best efforts while they were young.

Her overwhelming emotions were of disappointment and rejection. During the 1980s and '90s, many men from families settled in Britain sought a bride 'from home'. Phrases such as 'unspoilt country girl' were heard: a reaction to the alleged 'lax morals' of Western women, and even of women from South Asia brought up in the UK. By choosing an 'innocent' girl, it was thought, the happiness of the family would be assured. They were wrong: even the most 'simple' country girls proved to have minds of their own.

To make up for her sense of betrayal, Azma has given her boys everything. As a result debts have mounted, including significant rent arrears. Shafkhat is entitled to rent relief, since he is under 25. He refuses to sign on for Jobseeker's Allowance, being part of a growing cohort of young people endeavouring to find both a livelihood and a meaning in life outside a society and benefits systems in which they do not participate. This is the opposite of what the government wants to achieve: have they wondered whether deterring people from taking advantage of the scant welfare on offer may drive them, not into work, but into secret forms of elective outlawry?

Shafkhat was working with Amazon until three months ago. A back injury from a car crash prevented him from performing the tasks expected of him. There were days when he could not work at all. As a result, he was sacked. He is bitter about this, because, he says, he was about to be given a full-time contract, and was capable of packing orders faster than his co-workers. He spends most of his time at home, or at his auntie's house.

He says 'I would like to be a businessman, but that needs money.' Shafkhat will not sign on as unemployed, because he fears being pressured into work he does not want. He is not presently earning, but borrows from his mother or his working brother.

Azma has just been awarded a Personal Independence Payment (PIP) of £54.45 a week. She had been on an Employment and Support Allowance (ESA), but in view of her disability, she has been transferred to a support group. The PIP qualifies for a Carer's Allowance. Shafkhat has agreed to apply for this, since he and his two brothers make sure their mother is never left alone.

Azma has mountains of official correspondence that is unintelligible to her. She gathers up an armful of this opaque, hostile post, places it in her lap, and passes bits of it round for inspection. It appears that child support for the youngest boy has been stopped, even though, since he is at college, he is still entitled to it. The papers, a cascade of despair, are in disorder. Azma is apologetic: although she has lived here for 23 years, she has had little opportunity to learn English. She smiles at the neighbours, says 'How are you?' and 'It's a nice day'; but none of this is real communication.

It is no use ordering Azma to 'learn English'; where neither incentive nor opportunity has existed, it is too late for a woman in her mid forties, sick and partially disabled, to change her life. The boys have been her interpreters of the world; in the reverse relationship of migrants, the young become emissaries to and from the mysterious beyond of home and neighbourhood. Azma has made brief trips to Pakistan, mostly in celebration or in mourning.

Azma's life in Britain has been enclosed, not so different from the life she would have led in Pakistan, except for the absence of the network of family and kin. She has followed the prescribed role of raising her children. However much people of more 'enlightened' views may deplore the restriction of women to the home, this is the culture she has known and lived in, and to be evicted from it is a grievous loss. When her husband left her, she was not immediately thrown upon her own resources, since the State cushioned her against destitution. Now this is in retreat, and Azma is vulnerable as never before. The shrunken State also diminishes its citizens.

Shafkhat heard that his father is working and that his present wife also has a job. He never paid maintenance and the family never sought it – for reasons of reticence and shame. Technically, he owes his former wife a great deal. She will not claim it, and would not do so, even if her boys were not too proud to beg for restitution of what they missed as children. Male pride is no doubt real, but it is a luxury paid for by women.

Shafkhat will not engage with authority in any way. He has reluctantly been persuaded to be nominated as his mother's carer. To do so, he has to produce his last pay-slip and national insurance number; which, he feels, is a hostage to officialdom.

Disengagement from the agencies of the State is a dangerous form of alienation for young men, even though the State's dis-engagement from them – except in so far as it fears they may become 'radicalised' – is growing. Azma has brought up her boys to be good human beings. The oldest and youngest go to the mosque regularly, and she says *namaz* at home, but Shafkhat is less committed.

Azma's experience of Sialkot was another life: in north-east Punjab, in an ancient historic city where Damascene steel swords and knives were produced, from where older migrants to Britain still have the look of agriculturalists, with weather-beaten faces and eyes sharp from scanning the weather or pests on the crops. While they still have the air of displaced persons on the rubbish-strewn pavements of the West Midlands, their children have become different beings, urban, dependent upon the mobile phone – Shafkhat's rings incessantly – and divided from them by technology. Life is a mixture of modernity and tradition: the TV plays constantly, tuned to satellites that bring Pakistan into the heart of Britain, and a religion that has somehow become less merciful now than it was when people migrated here two or three generations ago.

Kareema

Kareema is more enterprising than many of her Muslim sisters. She has learned to survive and flourish alone. She is alert, intelligent and knowledgeable, not only about Islam, but also about the society into which she migrated 30 years ago.

Kareema has only the vaguest memories of her native Azad Kashmir. Her father came to Britain when he was 12 with his two grandfathers who were themselves cousins. They worked in the Bedford brickyards, at a time when men from South Asia were taking over from the Italians who, after the war, had been the principal source of brickyard labour.

Kareema was 'called over' when she was eight; she makes it sound as though she was summoned by destiny. There was then little support for immigrant children, and it took several years before she became fluent in English. 'I lived in a fog about the culture. I was treated as though I lacked intelligence because I couldn't speak the language properly. At home we spoke Mirpuri. Some children in the class were helpful, but in general I was ignored. You were left to your own devices, sink or swim. Fortunately, I could see that survival depended on taking control of my life. At that time people did not pick on Muslims simply for being Muslim. Now people are attacked for no other reason.'

Kareema's father was a fork-lift truck driver in the brickyards, and they had a four-bedroom house. They worked hard and pooled their earnings. Kareema was one of six children, four girls and two boys; another brother and a sister were born after they moved to Wolverhampton. As the eldest, Kareema was 'the pathfinder', a pioneer.

'I made all the mistakes, so my brothers and sisters could avoid them. At 16 I went back to Kashmir. Six months later I was married. I knew nothing. I didn't know how to do housework. It was a painful learning. None of my brothers or sisters went back to get married. I was the only one for whom a husband was found in Kashmir. That was how my parents had married, and they thought that was the way their children should follow. They chose him for me. It wasn't good. I did not tell my mother, I just kept it to myself.

'I came back to England for a year without him. It was hard to get his visa. It was rumoured my dad was offered land in return for the marriage. They called me for interview at the High Commission, to see if the marriage was genuine. Was your father offered land? They thought it was a fraudulent way to get my husband into Britain.'

When she returned to Kashmir, Kareema became pregnant. She didn't want a child. 'I was 19 when my daughter was born, and although I didn't like being pregnant, and didn't want his child, as soon as I saw her I realised she was also mine. She was beautiful and I fell in love with her straight away.'

It took more than six years for her husband to get a visa. In the meantime, she worked as overlocker in a sportswear factory. The pay was low and the hours long. She also did a child protection course. 'Everyone is now apparently most concerned about children; it is a pity that doesn't extend to the children of Gaza or Syria.

'When they first came, the two grandfathers and my father lived very frugally, all in one house, lots of people together, so they could save money to send home. It was the custom to marry cousins. Although my husband was also a cousin, this practice is declining now.

'He was very controlling. He ruled me, and wanted to direct everything I did – what I wore, where I went, how I looked, even the way I sat. It was as though I was his possession. It was a difficult life, and we were divorced. Actually, I divorced him. I was an independent woman. I told him from the start "Don't expect me not to talk back. I will, whatever you say." He couldn't take it. His was a very dominating personality. But I am not a woman to be dictated to.

'I am an observant Muslim. I'm strict. I choose to cover my head, but this is an open environment and I am my own person. I teach Arabic, the Quran, mainly to children. I enjoy it.

'The marriage lasted nine years. He didn't want to divorce. I had to go to the Sharia council. It took a long time before he would agree to sign. Not only that, he thought he could stop me marrying again, which he couldn't. I still see him. He is part of the family. His sister is in Wolverhampton; my mother and his mother are sisters, so our lives are intertwined; we see each other at weddings and funerals.

'I chose my second husband. He was originally a scientist. He used to teach, but he really wanted to be a writer. That marriage lasted five or six years. He became very religious. He ran a religious bookshop and community centre. Then he got married again without divorcing me. He wanted us all to live together, but she wouldn't. He became pious after we married and embraced polygamy. His new wife was a medical student. He didn't understand that women actually have feelings, so it would never have worked out, if we had even tried to live together in the same household.

'I have found the more experience you have, the more tolerant you become. I am religious. I started praying at 25, after I split up with my first husband. I started to think of the Creator, and I came to realise this life is nothing. This is not our real reason for living.

'I was not happy then. Working from eight in the morning till six at night in a factory, I had no time to pray or think. I felt something was missing in my heart. I started praying before my divorce. When I covered myself it brought peace to my heart.

'I had never learned my own religion. My family ruled, and I just accepted it. I began to pray for guidance. Our Muslim brothers and sisters think a woman cannot initiate a divorce, but she can. The subjection of women is cultural, not religious. You can wear a *hijab* and still do everything. You can be as independent as you choose.

'My family thought divorce was bad, particularly since I initiated it. They tried to keep us together. My mother did not have a mind of her own. She is very soft-hearted, and listens to everybody's advice. During the separation I had a nervous breakdown. For two weeks I did not speak. They thought their daughter had gone mad, because he had pressured me so much. Then they realised what he had done. They supported me then; but before that, they had been frightened: divorce, to them, meant the unravelling of life, and for a daughter to initiate it was against the natural order.

'I live with my son – he is 12, and from the second marriage. My first husband wanted my daughter to marry his older sister's son, her cousin. I said "No" – it would be the same pattern all over again. Before that, he had taken no interest in her, and never given any thought to her feelings. Then suddenly, he wants to revert to the old social custom. He has other children now.

'I have a house with three bedrooms. My daughter was doing accountancy, but didn't like it. She is now a carer in a private company on the minimum wage. Her ambition is to do social work.

'I used to work in the Asian Women's Community Centre, running an after-school club. Now I do home teaching, mainly Arabic, 16 hours a week, which also earns me tax credits.

'I have to pay the bedroom tax. If my daughter stayed with me, she would have to pay rent and council tax, so she has gone to stay with my mother. Bedroom tax is a lesser evil – £50 a month. It's only a box-room and there is no alternative accommodation. It is harsh and unjustified. They insist you do the impossible, then penalise you because you cannot do it. I have worked all my life. You pay a high price for being a single parent without being taxed extra for it. I bought a property when I was working, a house I kept for 12 years. I sold it before my second marriage, when I had my breakdown. I regret it now, but at that time I needed the money.'

Kareema has learned much from an experience bitterly acquired. She is respected in the community, since she teaches the Quran. Some judge her because she is a single parent; and because they have no father, her children are sometimes victims of prejudice. Kareema could not submit to the humiliations required of her for the social convention of staying with a husband she had no regard for.

Kareema knows the effects of migration on the spirit and psyche. Her father suffered depression and anxiety, and had periods in hospital. Her mother's family were never happy that they went to England. Close-knit families can offer support, but there is also jealousy in them, especially when property or money is involved. 'They split my mother and father up; especially my mother's mother and her sisters. Then they took over my father's property in Pakistan. It has been hard. It still is. But I have my faith and I have my children – the two greatest blessings.'

Born at the wrong time

In daily conversation it is common to hear older people say they would not want to be young now, since opportunities and life-chances for young people are diminishing. Despite constant technological innovation, and the promise of lives enhanced by improvements in communication, health care, entertainment and mobility, the experience of many young people has been one of narrowing horizons, instability and a degradation of employment. In the three months from February to April 2015, unemployment among 16- to

24-year-olds stood at 740,000, a rate of 16 per cent. Although this represented a decrease of about 100,000 over the previous year, many who have entered the labour market (or is it a bazaar?) are in temporary work, in make-work apprenticeships, on zero-hours contracts, or working part-time, often in jobs inimical to their inclinations and often well below their qualifications and intelligence. The government's conspicuous defence of pensioners – employing heroic rhetoric about those who have worked and saved all their lives and now deserve protection and security – has been largely at the expense of a new generation, which has been subject to much exhortation, moral lecturing and humbug, as well as mistreatment by the agencies of the State. In 2014, young people represented 27 per cent of those on Jobseeker's Allowance, yet they were victims of 43 per cent of the benefit sanctions imposed during that year. Government has become more severe. In March 2014, David Cameron asserted that 'order and discipline' had to be brought into their lives, and proposed 30 hours per week of community work for 18 to 21 year olds who were not in work, training or education, as a condition for receiving Youth Allowance, rather than Jobseeker's Allowance, although this would still remain at £57 a week. Among the 'duties' he proposed, as well as ten hours a week seeking work, were making meals for the elderly, cleaning graffiti, picking up litter and working with charities. It says much about the government's view of the world that working for 'the community' is seen as punishment and not as commitment to the common good.

Confirming this plan, in August 2015 the Conservative government renewed its attack upon a largely phantom 'embedded benefit culture', and declared its intention of imposing an 'intensive activity programme' upon 18- to

21-year-olds within three weeks of them submitting a claim for unemployment benefit. This, said Cabinet Office minister Matt Hancock, will 'end rolling welfare dependency for good', despite historical evidence that 'definitive' solutions to anything – particularly social and moral problems – are elusive, and often prove more damaging and costly than the evil they are supposed to 'cure'.

Young people between 18 and 21 are also to be denied housing benefit; an intervention which will evict an unknown number from independent living in hostels or rented flats. Those under 25 will be exempt from the so-called 'living wage', no doubt to encourage employers to take on more young people, thereby reducing the numbers not engaged in an occupation approved by the State.

The world of those uninvolved in education, work or training is largely unexplored. Many, without commitments and childless, are semi-detached, not only from the benefits system, in and out of which they move intermittently, but also from the 'mainstream' of society: an unhappy aquatic metaphor, with its connotation of dangerous currents.

Some avoid benefits altogether, finding other forms of economic activity and ways of making a living. Between June 2011 and March 2014, more than 1.9 million people on Jobseeker's Allowance had been sanctioned (many of them more than once). Forty-three per cent of these left Jobseeker's Allowance altogether; although some found jobs, a large number are unaccounted for, and left for what the Department for Work and Pensions calls 'other destinations' or 'unknown reasons'. Some will have turned to occupations that are on the borders of legality – hustling, selling prohibited or counterfeit goods, providing services and commodities outside the approved economy. Many live off others – family members in particular, often stretching the obligations of kinship to the limit. Peer-group friendships and petty crime nourish a secret economy of exchange, unofficial commerce, barter, selling and sex work. Those entangled in such activities often express contempt for the pitiful rewards of increasingly misnamed 'benefits', the receipt of which demands unacceptable and demeaning deference.

Significant numbers of young people are engaged in activities that might be illegal, but which provide them with a livelihood, sometimes precarious, occasionally lucrative – such as taking, dismantling and reassembling cars; buying and selling forged and stolen passports and visas; bribing officials and functionaries; dealing in contraband, false or stolen identities, smuggled goods, mobile phones and other electronic items disposed of at car-boot sales, fairs, festivals and weekly markets; commerce in small arms, knives and other weapons, or in drugs and pharmaceuticals including fake medicines. There is also the more familiar resort to cash-in-hand payments for services and skills that can be offered without arousing suspicion, such as performing in a band or organising the catering at unofficial events and parties. Social calm is, to some extent, maintained by the unmolested pursuit of a market that exists beyond the official statistics. A society which sets such high value on entrepreneurial virtues should not be surprised if these are sometimes exercised in shadowy, if not downright vicious, activities. For many people operating in this world, the benefits system scarcely exists, or furnishes too slender a living to be bothered with it; while others in the economic penumbra have been driven there by the failure of the welfare state to offer them the security it was meant to have provided for the weak and vulnerable, if not for the smart and opportunistic.

Young people have other disadvantages. They have been born into a world which advertises its wealth and promotes the desirability of all it produces so insistently that it seems society has been brought to such a degree of perfection there is no longer any room for improvement. This is a powerful disincentive to question the wisdom of the way things are. All a new generation can do is strive to be part of it; and only when, despite their best efforts, the bare bones of an unreconstructed system begin to show through the burnished appearances – indebtedness, the lack of affordable homes or of worthwhile occupations – does it become clear that many of the changes have been superficial, merely the politics of public relations, the surface paint of cowboy decorators.

Those who cannot avail themselves of the clandestine world of unofficial enterprise – the weak and sick, the timid and insecure – are the victims of welfare reforms; the smart and nimble avoid the system altogether. This is the greatest injustice of such reforms, since the innocent are punished in the absence of the unreachable, the dropped-out, the defaulters and dead souls of capitalism.

Abigail

Abigail had forgotten our appointment when I called. Her flat was chaotic and untidy, but she is a young woman of great warmth and charisma. Twenty years old, she lives in a housing association flat; an amenity that will be denied to under 21s after April 2017. This would expose her to even greater risks than those she took when she left home four years ago.

Abigail's family is from Zambia. She had been living in Reading with her mother, four siblings, and her aunt's five children, taken in when she could no longer care for them. The household was dramatically overcrowded, and Abigail wanted her independence. She left home at 16 and moved to Wolverhampton. 'Why Wolverhampton?' 'We lived here for a year when I was an early teenager. It was a mistake. They went back because they didn't like it. I did. I liked the friendliness of the people and the way they talked. When I first arrived, somebody said to me "You all right cock?" I said "What did you say?" I thought I was being insulted. It is just an expression.'

When Abigail left home, she simply took the train, and was met at the station by a friend she had made while at school in Wolverhampton. The friend knew two guys who lived in a house and had a spare room. They only wanted £10 a week for it. Abigail moved in and stayed for two months. Another friend, worried about her living in a house with two men, told her mother, who phoned the social services. They wanted to know what she was doing there.

'They thought the men were grooming me. "They're my friends." The social worker asked "How old are your friends? Where are they from? What do they do?" I said I didn't know, which was true. "We can't let a 16-year-old stay here with these men." They had told me they were 27 – one was 34 and the other 40. I told her I had never been touched. Social Services said it was what *might* happen if I stayed. They had fed me and I had paid next to nothing. I got very close to one of them: he had also left home at 17.

Social Services urged Abigail to go home. She refused. They found her a place in a hostel near the Young Offender Institution at Brinsford. She spent two and a half years there.

'It was not a good area. It was not safe. One girl was beaten up one day after she just went out to buy a bottle of milk.'

Abigail had no proof of her right to remain in Britain. In order to get Jobseeker's Allowance, the Department for Work and Pensions had to make sure she was here legally. She had left all her documents at home, including her passport, not expecting to have to show her papers when travelling in Britain. It took nine months before she could access benefits. In the meantime, she received help from the Church, and her key worker provided food. 'You learn to make do with leftovers. I got a parcel every Thursday from the Church – cereal, canned meat and vegetables, sachets of soup. You couldn't choose. If you were lucky, you might get a tin of peaches.

'I had a bedroom and a living room in the hostel, but nothing, no TV, and I knew no one. I used to go to one of the guys down the hall if I wanted to watch TV. I realised how terrible it was one day, when I found I hadn't even got the bus fare to get to the city centre. I was crying and asking "What have I done to myself?" My key worker helped with the Home Office to prove I had the right to stay in the country and was entitled to benefit. My brother sent proof we had been here for 15 years. Still they delayed. In the end I got back pay of £500.

'My mother had worked in the UK as a nurse in the health service. She went back and forth to Zambia, until she could bring us all here. I was very young, only three, so I have little memory of the place. I remember my grandparents, but my life has been here. I feel English.

'The people at the Jobcentre are ignorant. Last year, my nan died. I was on benefit, and due to sign on the day after she died. I asked them "Can I sign on the day before?" "You have to come to your appointment or lose your benefit." They take the piss.'

Despite the obstacles placed in the way of young claimants, Abigail proved enterprising and tenacious. At 17 she was receiving benefit, and at 18 transferred to Jobseeker's Allowance. She got Income Support because she went to college to study music. She didn't finish the course, because a friend, a singer with a band, told her they were looking for another singer. Her college tutors advised her to go for it. It seemed the kind of break she'd dreamt of.

'We were promised the earth, but finished up with next to nothing. I was still on Jobseeker's Allowance and staying in the hostel. I can sing, and I still hope for a singing career. When we started, we had just three days to learn an hour's stuff. The guy running it, Seb, said he had his own company, but we didn't see any money.

'We did a lot of gigs for a year. We were promised £500 a gig, but with three singers, two girls and a boy, and split three ways, it wasn't much. We were paid bits and pieces, but it never amounted to anything near what we expected. Seb showed us the books – we had gigs at clubs, festivals, events. It really affected me – this was what I wanted to do in life. I was 18 and I'd left college for what I thought was a career. I did get a qualification from college. I could have done better but for the distraction of chasing a career that didn't happen.

'I went by chance to Connexions [a careers and advice service for young people]. I had moved out of the hostel by that time, and was living here. I had no TV, no carpet, practically no furniture. I had a flat that I couldn't live in. Gradually, I got some stuff together, and even if it's a bit untidy, it's my own. It costs £300 a month. I get housing benefit, but pay £20 a month towards council tax. I'm struggling to pay off debts. I'm surviving. In a hostel, you have no responsibility. All you had to do was find your own food. Here, there is electricity, water, that's £25 to £30 for two weeks. I need the internet to apply for jobs. Then there's the TV licence. My brother pays my mobile phone bill. I get £100 a fortnight. It used to be £114, but they reduced it since they started taking council tax out of it.

'I eat one meal a day, chicken and rice. I cook – I get 20 pieces of chicken for £2 from Asda, so I'll buy 40 for £4 and a big bag of rice that will last. I buy spices when I have money. I eat fruit when I can. I buy eggs, bread, juice. No milk. I like pizza.'

Abigail's kitchen was poorly supplied with nourishment. Young people starve their bodies to feed their dreams. The energy and commitment with which they pursue their ambitions is moving, even though their dreams often finish up in the same famished state as their bodies. They know what they want, and are ready to run all risks, against which welfare no longer offers a reliable cushion.

'I have debts – arrears of about a thousand pounds. I have to go to the County Court to get the amount I'm paying in arrears reduced. I'm paying £17 a fortnight, and I hope they'll reduce it to £6. One of my brothers is a great help. He goes to Uni, but is working as well. The rest of the family have gone their ways – married, they have their own lives.

'I've been threatened with eviction three times. I couldn't bear to lose this place. You don't realise how terrible homelessness is until you've had a place of your own.

'My boyfriend stayed for a year. He was the best one I'd ever had. At least, that's how it was at the start. It was all good. It took me some time to realise what a psycho he was. He hit me, he abused me. I couldn't go out. It began like, he wanted to do everything for me, so I didn't need to go anywhere. I said "I want to go out." "No, I'll do it, I'll go to the shops, I'll get whatever you want." But what he wanted was total control.

'I met him in the hostel. I knew his brother and the brother's girlfriend, so it was not as if he was a stranger. But he was possessive. I was working at Marks and Spencer's. He came in late, about one in the morning. I was fast asleep. I had to get up for an early shift the next day. He woke me up and said he wanted to talk about his feelings. Just what I needed. He wasn't drunk. He did smoke weed, but he hadn't been smoking it that day. I said "I've been up since seven, working. Let's talk tomorrow." No, he wanted to talk there and then. When I said no, he punched me in the face. As a result I needed hospital treatment. He pushed me and banged my head against the wall. I was in shock.

'Afterwards, I was in and out of consciousness. I managed to phone my friend Chloe. She asked "Have you been hit?" "No, I fell downstairs." I didn't want to admit it. Chloe said "We have to go to A and E." Later, he came back as though nothing had happened. He wanted me to feel I was the crazy one. He said to Chloe "Are you taking Abbie to hospital because I hit her?" Then he asked "Have you got a fag?" as though everything was normal.

'But it was the way he said it – it seemed he was proud of having knocked me about. Chloe came with me to the hospital. My nose had been dislocated, but it wasn't broken. They said "You are a lucky lady – somebody must be looking down on you." One more punch, it would have damaged my brain.

'I stayed with him for another couple of months. I thought "I can't let him drive me out of my home." It was never the same after that. In the end, I said "Don't let us kid ourselves." He moved out at the end of last year.

'I have to go to the Jobcentre, check in with my adviser, who looks at all the places I've applied to since our last meeting. I have an interview tomorrow with Homeserve. When you are desperate, you'll take anything. I worked in a Caribbean take-away. I was that broke, I worked 12 hours a day. I was promised £60 a night. The owner often didn't pay. Once he gave me just £12 for a 12-hour shift. One pound an hour.

'It is still my dream to be a singer. I can't give up now I've had a taste of it.'

Adele and Clifford

A flat in a small modern block just off the ring road: an area landscaped with berberis and cotoneaster. *Adele* and *Clifford* live on the first floor. This is difficult for Adele who, when she wants to go out, has to go downstairs on her backside, because she cannot bear any pressure on her feet. She suffers from pustular psoriasis, with persistent outbreaks of blisters on hands, arms and feet. 'They tell me it is a result of stress, with an element of allergy. It started eight months ago. It coincided with money worries. I also got hit by a car which broke my foot. I was doing a catering job, and it was not easy to work walking on crutches.

'I was also a carer for my ex-husband, who was disabled. After I split up with him, I was desperate for a job. I got a position as chef in a restaurant close to West Park.'

Clifford was also in catering. He was officially a chef, but expected to do everything, including clean up food spilt on the floor. It was, he said, his first proper job. Adele is 24 and Clifford 23.

Adele's husband left her before they had been married a year. He was in a wheelchair and suffered from a disorder of the nervous system. He left her heavily in debt, which she had to pay after the divorce, because the credit cards were in her name. 'To be left owing £5,000 at the age of 19 would shake anyone's confidence. He took most of the furniture from the flat, so when I met Cliff, we could get no credit and had nothing. I was evicted from the flat I had shared with my husband. Since the car accident I've been on Tramadol, an opiate drug for pain relief.'

Adele's family lives in Dudley. She rarely asks her parents for help, because her mother looks after her sick father and also Adele's 18-year-old brother, who is autistic but 'very bright'. Sometimes Adele's grandfather gives them a few pounds.

Clifford and Adele have been together for three years. He is her carer, because she cannot do anything without assistance. She is heavy, and in her present condition must be helped to wash, dress and use the toilet.

'We have been sanctioned by the Department for Work and Pensions, and stuck without money for weeks on end. The council helped with food parcels. We have one meal a day. Cliff sometimes misses a meal so I can eat, or we buy a meal for one and split it into two.

'I am on Employment and Support Allowance which is £343 every two weeks. Housing benefit and council tax are covered. We save on food, because we have Sky TV, and Cliff has his Xbox. We have mobile phones, because they are part of life. At the moment, we don't have a TV licence.

'We don't eat breakfast. We just eat dinner at six o'clock. Tonight it is cheese and potato pie. Yesterday, we had a pork dinner. Cliff got eight pork chops for £4 – food for four days. Of course, you get fed up having the same thing all the time – our main stand-by is pasta bake.' Cliff eats apples but Adele will not eat fruit, unless it is in juice form. 'We get tinned vegetables, frozen broccoli and cauliflower. We have fresh carrots which are cheap at the moment. Opinions vary about diet when you have psoriasis. Some say don't eat dairy products or bread; but we don't have much of either anyway. I've never worried about nutrition – I was brought up on takeaways, chips and pizza.'

Food occupies a prominent place in the conversation of hungry people. Their consumption limited, they entertain fantasies about what they would like to eat if they could afford it. It is no use advising people to 'eat healthily', particularly when so much of contemporary life depends on things other than food – mobile phones, tablets, PCs, DVDs. In order to participate in society (and the economist Amartya Sen defines the contemporary poor as those unable to participate in customary social activities), young people give priority to what sterner observers might regard as luxuries: these are indispensable for social contact, especially for those cut off from the world.

'I am still paying off my debt, waiting for the debt agencies to co-ordinate it. We have 12 company debts between us; and Cliff has a debt to Speedy Cash, an American loan company that lends instant money.'

Clifford says: 'I used to work in the Rubicon Casino, valet, serving food and drinks, and helping in the kitchen. I worked there a year. I loved it. It was good money and I was meeting people. But my then relationship broke down and I lost my job. I was under a lot of pressure – I was doing the work of at least two people. I couldn't take it. My managers couldn't sort it out, so I left. I also had problems with my family and ended up on the streets.

Clifford slept on Pelsall Common in Walsall. He survived on custard cream biscuits. He slept outside for more than six months, including winter. At the same time, he found it strangely relaxing. It made him calmer. There were no money worries. He kept warm by building a shelter out of twigs and branches. He loved the wildlife, birds and animals, watching the foxes. It took his mind off other things. He survived by stealing bicycles, selling them on or just for scrap.

'I grew up in a house where there were always arguments. It was rough and it affected me. My mother loved me, but not my father. As a child, he beat me. I am by nature a quiet person, but if anything upsets me, I can become very aggressive. I still feel a lot of anger against my father. I was scared of him. If I said anything to my mother he would start on her.

'My father knew Adele's mum from school. When he found out we were together, he called her family everything under the sun. When my family were in difficulties, we gave them money. Not even a thank you. Then, when it gets near to Christmas, they suddenly want to know you again.

'My dad has seen how I have turned out, and now he is scared of me. He got the police on to me once, and I was fined for being drunk and disorderly. I was actually protecting my mother. When I lose my temper, I can be very aggressive. Inside, I have all the aggression my father showed to me. Last year, a neighbour attacked me with a knife, slashed my face. You can see the scar. He came at me with a kitchen knife. He is now in a psychiatric hospital. The whole landing here was covered in blood. It looked like a massacre.'

Adele needs a ground-floor flat, since she uses a wheelchair to move around, even indoors. She has not been outside for six weeks. Her medication weakens her immune system, so while it helps the psoriasis, it makes her vulnerable to infection. She must not get pregnant with psoriasis.

'They couldn't diagnose it. It began a year ago. My GP thought it was scabies, then dermatitis, and only when I went to the hospital I learned what it was. I don't ask much of life – to be able to walk out of that door, be able to wear socks and shoes, and eventually, go back to work.' Adele's desire – like that of many people incapacitated or impoverished – is modest; but at present, it is an impossible dream.

'On good days I enjoy life. I read somewhere that you should live each day as though it were your last. For us, a good day means scrimping on food so we will be able to eat better tomorrow. A birthday treat is to have breakfast. Somebody gave Cliff a bottle of whisky for Christmas, but normally we don't drink.'

Adele was assessed for a Personal Independence Payment. Twelve points are required to get the enhanced rate, and this will also entitle her to a carer. If it fails, Cliff will be forced to work. He was doing a course at the Further Educational College on Security. He was late one morning, because he had to help Adele use the toilet. 'They said "Don't bother to come in anymore."'

Cliff is a thoughtful, intense young man. He finds comfort in the countryside. We talk about climate change. He says 'Well, it's Mother Nature, isn't it? We are destroying the earth and she is paying us back. You have to expect to receive what you give.'

He also admits to writing poetry – half-ashamed as though it were a sign of weakness.

Adele was granted the higher rate of independence payment, and Cliff is her official carer. They have a more secure income, but accumulated debts from the past are not easily paid off.

Benefit 'sanctions' appear to their victims as gratuitous cruelty; and if official denials of any punitive intent in the formulation of policy are true, it suggests that local administrators have been given some incentive to save money and some discretion to exercise, not leniency, but severity. They are thereby continuing a long tradition of State functionaries, from overseers of the poor and Poor Law administrators, to workhouse masters and means-test men.

Graham Chinnery: zero hours

Graham is one of the 50 per cent of graduates who, it was reported in 2015, are working below their qualifications (*Guardian*, 19 August). Born on a poor estate in Wolverhampton, he lived with his parents and brother until he went to university. He defines his family as 'working class'.

'We had no holidays, no car and lived in rented property. My father has been a bin-man all his life, and my mother is a health-care assistant. She was a machinist in a clothing factory, and that was when she met my father. Both have always worked; very much part of the "respectable" working class. They hate people on benefits: they see them as lazy scroungers. They are a good example of George Osborne's "people who do the right thing". Their attitude is contradictory, because my brother, now 30, has been unemployed all his adult life.'

People make exceptions for those they know and love, understanding that their circumstances require tenderness in dealing with their needs. It is always 'the others', people unknown, who are the cheats and shirkers.

'My brother has a mental health problem. He is quite reclusive. As a teenager, he lacked confidence. I think he suffers from agoraphobia. Our parents do not push him. Whatever is wrong is undiagnosed. It's kept in the family.'

Graham found home emotionally draining and left as soon as he could. 'They pretend nothing is happening, it is all part of a normal pattern.' He used to have rows with them, but has given up such fruitless disputes. His brother has no relationships, but watches TV and spends hours online. Graham shared a room with him, which he found irritating.

Graham never told people where he came from: the name of the estate would tell them more than he wanted them to know. He was the first in his family ever to go to university. At school he was pushed. His brother was never an achiever, and the hopes of his parents were poured into him. They were proud, but he felt under-appreciated. 'When I was doing my A levels, I was working 20 hours a week in McDonald's and studying at the same time. My brother had stopped education at 16, was out of school and doing nothing. He went into a social hibernation from which he has never emerged. I now feel shame over my own embarrassment. I said horrible things to my mother when I was younger, like "It's your fault." I regret it now.

'My parents have a great relationship. My father is an intelligent man. His father walked out on the family when he was 13, and he became the de facto father to the three younger brothers and sister. His mother did two jobs. When he was young, he had trials as a professional footballer. Although he didn't make it, he is not bitter. It is heart-breaking – what might have been; but that is the story of many working-class people. He talked politics to me when I was young. I knew all about current affairs. I ought to have studied politics.

'I got a degree in journalism. English was my strongest subject. I also did media studies, TV, film and culture. I never wanted to be a 1970s-type notebook reporter. I am attracted to radio, and did a placement with Wolverhampton BBC, doing interviews for the archive.

'After university, I stayed in Manchester for a time, then came back to Wolverhampton. I was signing on and claiming benefit. I lived with a friend who, it turned out, had forged the tenancy agreement on the flat. I got called up for a benefits investigation. I was accused of fraud and had to pay £350. My mother came with me to the investigation. They try to get under your skin, but I stayed cool and co-operative.

'Since then I've worked in market research, all on zero hours. I've spent four years in offices working the phones. The only other employment was a few months working with my uncle, a roofer. That was brilliant because you got cash in hand. I felt proud, like I was "doing a man's job", manual labour, working class. But he was a slave driver, I couldn't keep up. Another time I worked in a cinema. All the employees – except the manager – had high-class degrees – engineering, psychology, journalism. We joked that if the world came to an end, between us, we would survive on the skills we had.

'One zero-hours company paid £6.50 an hour, another £7.50. The highlight of my career was £8.20, but that included holiday pay. There is no job security, but it does give you a certain freedom. It serves the company's needs first – most people would trade it for a fixed contract. There are no disciplinary procedures, just dismissal. A friend who complained there were no breaks in a four-hour stint was gone the next day. We were allowed to spend ten minutes in four hours not dialling, and that included lavatory breaks. That was called "idle time".

'I worked for companies conducting customer satisfaction surveys, asking whether people were happy with services they had received – engineers, home service, housing repairs. That's the easy end of the spectrum, because you're following up on services already provided, not canvassing for work or selling anything. It is supremely boring, but not harrowing.

'I'm leaving Wolverhampton after the summer. I'm going to Europe to be near my girlfriend. I'll be teaching English as a foreign language in Austria. I will always think of Wolverhampton as home. Most of my friends are here – I was the only one to go to Uni. Most of those I was at school with are still living with their parents, but all are working – offices, restaurants, factories or labouring on building sites. They are in relatively well-paid employment. I sometimes think I'd have done better not to go on to higher education. I don't regret it, but in terms of career, it did nothing for me.'

There were 50 students on Graham's journalism course: of these, three are working in the media. Most are working in Asda or Debenhams, in bars and kitchens or sandwich shops. It raises questions about the value of education: its implicit promise you'll get some sort of career. Many young people feel they've been conned, and are deep in debt into the bargain. 'It may make you a better citizen', says Graham, 'but there is no guarantee you'll ever earn enough to pay back the debts you've piled up.'

Education, imposed upon the working class in the 1870s, met resistance from those who thought keeping their children at school would damage their capacity to earn and to contribute to family income. The education of many clever children of modest means was curtailed at the statutory school-leaving age for the same reason (age 10 in 1880, 11 in 1893, 12 in 1899, 14 in 1918, 15 fully implemented only in 1947 and 16 in 1972). With the vast expansion of higher education in the mid and late twentieth century, education was transformed, not into necessary training for industry, but as a doorway to the opportunities opened up in post-industrial society. The new employment structure of the twenty-first century no longer sharply demarcates the highly educated from those caught in work without prospects. Graham is at the end of an assurance of advantage to those who study to degree level. This diminution of life-chances, which, it seemed, would grow indefinitely, has reduced the horizons of a new generation, with consequences we have yet to see.

Andrea

Andrea lives in a two-bedroom flat with her two dogs. She calls them her 'children'; at least for the present, since, in order to have real children, she will need IVF treatment. 'You also need a partner, which I have; but he doesn't live with me.'

Andrea, 24, has two dreams: the first, to become a youth worker, the second, a mother. That such elementary desires should become 'dreams' says much about the artificially induced privation in which people live.

'My partner is on a zero-hours contract with the TK Maxx distribution centre. He has had no work for three weeks. He lives at home with his mother, brothers and sisters. When he stays over, I make a meal, but that all costs money. I was getting £114 a fortnight, but it's now cut to £89. I am on work placement, but I had to take a budgeting loan from the Social Fund, which I am paying back.

'I spend £9 a fortnight on water, £20 on electricity and £20 a fortnight on food. I buy potatoes, milk and bread – four loaves, and freeze three of them. I'll eat mash, gravy and sausages or make a pasta sauce and freeze half of it. My partner loves cooking. We go to Morrisons at closing-time and get little treats on their sell-by date. I'm also paying £20 on my tumble-dryer – I need it for clothes, in case I get an interview: you have to look your best. It's expensive, applying for jobs, because you also have to pay for travel. I have £10 for smokes and extras. I smoke roll-ups when I have nothing to eat, because it cuts the appetite and keeps me calm. Music also helps. I like Celine Dion, Michael Jackson, Whitney Houston, not rock music or opera. If I go out – which is rare – I love karaoke. The only regular place I go is to Bingo at the Gala, which is free on Mondays and Thursdays. My biggest win was £50.'

Andrea grew up in Birmingham, but moved out because there 'it's all fighting and drugs'. Here, life is peaceful. Andrea has four brothers and one sister, but is in close contact only with her oldest and youngest brothers. All have the same mother, but she and her young brother have the same father, and the older brothers have another.

It is sometimes difficult to follow the kinship relations in networks of divorce and remarriage, the garnering of other people's children in domestic groupings called 'family units'. Andrea's biological father remarried. He forbade her to see her half-brothers and sisters. She regards her half-sister as her closest sibling, but they meet in secret.

'My mother remarried when I was two. But then he – that is, my stepfather – cheated on her with her sister; and he married her, my auntie.

'I was abused as a child. An uncle on my stepfather's side. I was eight or nine. I never told my mother about it until I was 16. People sometimes tell me I act like a child: if I do, it's because my childhood was stolen from me. I grew up too soon. I knew it was wrong, what he was doing, but I didn't have the strength to say anything. When you are a victim of adults, you think they know best, and in any case, no one would believe you, especially if it is a relative. You carry that with you all your life.'

These stories of sexual violence against children are now more readily believed; and the pursuit of offenders has become more assiduous. But the emphasis is on bringing perpetrators to 'justice', while the damaged children have become adults; and the harm they have suffered is rarely taken into account by society, by the benefits system, by employers, by their peers and neighbours, even though many have been left with a sense of worthlessness, guilt, fear and distrust of others. None of this enters into consideration of people's 'employability': their economic function is detached from their humanity, since this, and their capacity to earn, is all that the crude instruments of economic 'well-being' are designed to measure.

'I struggled at school. I did child care, going from nursery to nursery. I didn't like it. I wanted to do youth work. I like young people from 12 to 18. I volunteered in a youth club in Birmingham, which I loved. I even carried on after I moved to Wolverhampton. I like children, but I don't want to look after them as a job. I baby-sit for a friend of my mother every weekend, which helps with a bit of cash.

'I've had a dramatic life. I drank some turpentine when I was very small, because it had been left in a lemonade bottle. Then I jumped out of a window. I was drinking heavily at 16. The police picked me up in a park. They actually helped me to start a new life.

'I worked at Amazon, where I met my partner. I fell in love with him on my very first day. I earned good money. It didn't last, because I had to go into hospital with a problem of the womb, where I found out I would have to have IVF if I wanted children. After that, the company wouldn't take me back. It isn't fair. You should not be penalised for ill health which is not your fault.

'I put on a good front, but behind closed doors I cry a lot. I ask myself why I am here. At the beginning of the year I wanted to end it. I was going to throw myself under a train, but I couldn't, because it is not fair to the people who love me.

'My best friend was my grandfather. He used to play with me when I was a child. We would play checkers and go out together. He gave me security. Since he died, I have lost three or four friends, all young. One died of a heart attack. One was killed in a knife crime, and the other in a car accident – he went straight into a tree. I couldn't go to any of the funerals. I think I hadn't grieved properly for my granddad, and that is why I couldn't face going to anyone else's funeral. I am a ticking time-bomb: there are many unresolved issues from my childhood. I don't really have friends here. If you have been abused, it destroys your trust in people. I see my brother; we play PlayStation together. Life is a struggle for him too. He is also in rent arrears because of the bedroom tax.

'He borrows from my mum for food. She works as a carer in a home. But she is not in good health – she can't put pressure on her feet, and can't do the 12-hour shifts they expect. She got stitched up by her ex-partner, who left her with bills, including a £600 council tax bill.

'I want to work. I can't get tax credits till I'm 25. I had my first job before it was legal to work. I earned £500 a month and I thought I was rich. I was a trainee at McDonald's, but I was up against a Polish girl, and she got the permanent job.

'I take my dogs out every day. One is a cross between a husky and a snow-dog. He's called Oscar. I call him "Son". If I'm not well, he won't leave me. He has his own bedroom. I will spend on them at Christmas.

'I've also chosen the names of my children, when I have them. If I have a boy, he will be Tyler James – James after my grandfather. If it's a girl, Caitlin.'

Carl Hendricks

Carl, 22, is an energetic, ambitious young man. Born in Handsworth, Birmingham, he pays tribute to his mother who, he says, 'did a good job in bringing me up. There was no father. Well, there was, but he was in Jamaica, which is where they met. She had gone back home and came back to Wolverhampton with me in her belly. My father did come to this country in 1998, but never lived with us.

'I grew up around gang culture. My brother was part of it. He is now 33. I have a sister of 32 and a brother of 30. My oldest brother is in prison. When I was small, I used to think he was my dad. I must have been six or seven before I realised he wasn't. We had different fathers, so when I heard them talking about Dad, Dad, I thought he must be mine. When you are young, you can't work things out. You're in a world over which you have no control.

'I sometimes see my father now. He grew up in Spanish Town, a poor part of Kingston. He was a painter and worked on house maintenance for a housing association in East London. He always worked and he advised me to do the same. My father got legal status, but one uncle was deported, caught carrying bullets near Heathrow. My father doesn't read or write.

'One of my brothers and my sister have the same father. Another brother has a different one; and I have yet another one. When you are born into this world, you have no choice of your parents or your identity. Nobody ever asks to be born.

'My mother's mother died when mum was 13. Mum struggled. She is now 50, and was manager of a pub. At 46, she decided to go back to study, to get maths and English. Now she fosters children. She gave me a good upbringing. My auntie worked at Tesco's for ten years. She was also offered a manager's job, but turned it down because she can't read or write.

'I was never keen on school, because of all the things going on around me. I've got my dad's blood. He is a hustler. By the time I was in year seven at school, I was already working – gardening, car-washing, earning a bit here and there. I was never in school, and when I was, I was always being suspended for messing about.

'I have been to Jamaica a few times. There, if you say anything wrong, it can cost you your life. Their mind is different. They just live life. I am happy to be English. I want to do things differently. I don't want to have kids young – you see kids having kids.

'I wanted to leave home. I felt a need to go and get away, start my own life. I went to live in a hostel. A terrible place – kids who had been abused, addicts, into self-harm. I had never seen people who cut their skin before. It was like a jail. You came out of there an addict or a pusher or a mother. I stayed nine months.

'My big brother had practically moved out by the time he was 14. He was selling weed as a kid, that was his generation. When he came out of prison last time, he was taken up by a woman who was quite well off. He went to live with her, but said he didn't want to be a house-husband, and took off.

'He has been in and out of prison. The first time he was locked up was in 2003, when he was 18. It comes from my father's side of the family – it's expected, almost a tradition. If I had stayed at home, being the youngest, I would have been used as a baby-minder. I wanted to go where they had no power over me. The family puts people into a mess. They can mess you over 20 times, and will carry on till you go into your grave.

'My brother phoned. "I need money." I think "Go and work for it." He won't sign on. He lives off people. He lived with me last time he came out. Armed police came to the house. He took my car, and blackmailed the family into helping him.

'By the age of 18 I had my own flat. I was lucky. I had a six-month apprenticeship, working four days a week for £30. I was also selling drugs. Chase the money. It was exciting. I only stopped that about a year ago. I was making money, on the road day and night. I would go to bed at four o'clock in the morning.

'The police raided my house. They came every day, nine of them. They were wearing long coats. I thought 'Why are they dressed like that?' They had guns inside the coat. In my house they found two fake guns. I was scared. I went to the police station. Nothing else happened. But they used to watch me. I was only selling weed. Earlier, I used to sell crack. I also was a gambler. A friend of mine once made seven grand in a week.

'I was lucky. I met an older Jamaican guy, who literally saved me. I had guidance from him. He has wisdom. He helped me, became a sort of father-figure. At the same time, I got an apprenticeship and got a Level One in Sport, coaching basketball. Then I did another course, this time in painting and decorating. I want to go back and do my GCSEs again, because at school I got a D in English and an E in Maths. I need to change that. I don't know yet what I want to do. My brother's dad owns a record label – I could work, selling, for him. With my older friend, we are trying to set up a business, printing T-shirts. We have a printer and I am setting up a website. I have a business plan. I have a lot of energy. I want to get on with life.

'I'm also working with another friend, a journalist, and we are writing a book together, the story of my family. I am collecting their experiences which we're going to turn into fiction. I have a lot of possibilities. There is much more to life than drugs and hustling. I've discovered that before it's too late.

'I signed up for Universal Credit. It used to be Jobseeker's Allowance. But then I just got a job at a warehouse, Saturday and Sunday nights. I get £104 for two nights' work. I get £53 housing benefit, which leaves £29 for me to pay. That leaves me with £74 a week. It's a start; but only a start.'

In August 2015, Carl was transferred to Universal Credit. The aim of this reform is to merge six unemployment and in-work benefits into one. Implementing this has been a slow process, mainly because of the complexity of people's shifting circumstances. It has begun with single people, whose life-changes are easier to track than, say, those of two adults with children. In its early stages, 70 per cent of claimants were male and a majority (53 per cent) under 25. The theory of Universal Credit is that it will enable people to get into work, and eventually to avoid State support altogether: as they earn more per hour or increase their working hours, this will ultimately enable them to 'escape' poverty. As a mechanism for poverty-abatement it is highly questionable, since when George Osborne announced in November 2015 that he had cancelled the cuts to tax credits, what he did not say was that much of the revenue anticipated from those cuts would be recuperated from rates of Universal Credit, which will be lower than working tax credits. Nor will it help people to leave part-time or casual labour for permanent work, or compel employers to pay above a minimum wage, even when transformed by an official alias into a 'living' wage.

Arif Hossein

Arif is now in his late twenties. His story illuminates the path many young people have taken in a search for identity and meaning in a world where conflicting 'choices' trap them in lives they do not want, and situations which can lead to jail or to the embrace of apocalyptic values, and increasingly, to both.

When Arif came out of prison for his part in an attempted robbery on a post office, he signed on as unemployed. It took ten months to find work. 'The Jobcentre staff told me not to let employers know I had been in prison. I couldn't do that, because they would find out and then I'd be out of work again. The purpose of the Jobcentre was to get people into employment at any price.

'My father was old when I was born. He was born in Rawalpindi in 1925, in what was then part of undivided India. He died in 2012: his life spanned partition, independence and migration. His own father had come from Ghazni in Afghanistan, capital of the first Muslim dynasty in Afghanistan, which extended to Persia and North India; so we were originally of Persian heritage. My grandfather died when my father was seven. He was brought up by his mother and his father's sister. He had to leave education as a child and work. He used to pick up old cigarette packets and use them to practise writing and maths. He joined the army when he was 17. He went into the Medical Corps and studied at Rawalpindi Medical College. He helped the casualties of Partition in 1947.

'My father came here in the 1950s. After the War, people who had been in the army were welcomed to work and to become citizens. They were invited. My father was in a textile factory in Dewsbury in Yorkshire, labour that helped keep the textile mills open. They soon closed down anyway. He came alone, although he was married and had one son – my half-brother. I have never met him, but he must also be quite old by now. My father's wife died and the boy was looked after by relatives. He never came to England. My father went back to Rawalpindi, met my mother and married her. He wanted to bring his son here. He completed all the paperwork, but one of my father's cousins was jealous that my father had come to England. So when the papers came, the cousin ripped them up. As a result, he never came. My father was heartbroken. The next time his son saw him was when his casket was being lowered into the ground.

'When my father died, the family – my mother, two sisters and brother – went to the funeral. I couldn't go because my passport had expired. He was 86. He had Parkinson's, dementia and heart problems.

'My two sisters and brother were born in Dewsbury. When my mother was pregnant with me, the National Front was very active in Yorkshire. They attacked houses and beat people up. They threw a brick through our window one night, and it missed my mother by inches. So they came to London to my mother's sister, and I was born in London.

'We never had a home in London. My mother fell out with her sister and we couldn't stay there. Other members of the extended family lived in Wolverhampton, so this was the logical place to come. My father worked in a factory here. Migration for him meant downward social mobility. He had become a medical auxiliary in the Pakistani army, but here, he was an unskilled labourer.

'I was good at school. I got a place in university. But I fell in with a bad crowd and did stupid things.'

By the time he was 14 or 15, Arif was smoking cannabis and was soon selling drugs. When he went to university – to study music and sound engineering and production – he maintained contact with his friends, who were making a lot of money. Arif says he 'dropped out'; a rather evasive formula that makes it sound as though it were a kind of accident. 'I felt out of place in university. All my friends were on the street, selling drugs or passing counterfeit money, fake £20 notes, which you could exchange at petrol stations for real ones. Some owners who were not willing to take them we bullied into it. We levied an unofficial tax on filling stations, restaurants and other businesses; the guys involved were from Birmingham, Manchester and Bradford.

'Mine was a good family. I am a Muslim and was brought up to know right from wrong. I knew what Islam was, but I was not following it. I was aware of what was going on, and I noticed when Islam got radical. You couldn't miss it, because people were giving talks in mosques and at meetings, where they would pump you up. They showed videos of women and children being killed in Palestine and Iraq. You could feel how it appealed to young people. I had been taught that Allah is with those who are patient. Young people were told Muslims had been patient. Some of the radicals said 9/11 was a righteous cause. If anyone presented a version of Islam to people who were in gangs and on the streets, where violence was accepted, they would not have to change very much, and the transition would be easy. In Islam submission to Allah is central; these people were asking for submission to a violent cause; and those who followed them would not have to give up anything: they could carry on robbing and scamming and thieving, to fund "the cause", jihad, or whatever it was called. The implication was that it was OK for kids to stick people up in the streets, grab mobile phones, deal in cannabis or cocaine. The money was cleansed through legitimate business – car rental places, taxi services, and therefore it was also morally cleansed because it was serving "religion".

'I was not a good Muslim. I smoked and drank. Someone decided on a break-in at a post office and off licence. It was quick money, take out the booze and sell it fast. I was with them. The plan was to break in from behind the building. We didn't know people were living in the flats above. I had a bad feeling about it. I said "Don't let's do it." But I couldn't back out. It would have looked like a betrayal. So I stayed.

'The couple living in the building heard us and called the police. A police car came, no light, no siren. I said "Come on, let's get out quick." There were six of us. I was last to leave the building. I and one other guy were caught by the cops, taken to the police station and questioned. The good thing is that I admitted it. I said I didn't know any of the others. I had no previouses.

'I was tried and went to prison. I was 22. I got 14 months, on appeal reduced to seven, because I was of good character. I actually had a change of heart even before the post office job. I had gone back to Uni to do a degree, this time in accountancy. Going to prison made it impossible to finish it. That made two unfinished degrees.

'I had already met people who were into Sufism and meditation. I love the poetry of Rumi. I am a poet and musician myself, and Rumi lit that up inside me. It was as though something had been dormant, and came to creative life.

'In prison, I met a guy who had been a hit-man for 15 years. He was serving a long sentence. But he became a Muslim and was also into Sufism. But then he joined a hard-core radical group. Although we both took the same side, we followed quite different paths.

'As I see it, Muslims in Britain have genuine grievances. They feel segregated, excluded. They see black youngsters who are into gangs and drugs. Some young Muslims start down this path. Then they come to a crossroads, where you either get deeper into the gang and drug culture, or you transfer the feelings of aggression and anger into a form of apparently religious salvation. But they are the same: neither leads to peace or satisfaction. This guy I was in prison with got caught up with these people who preach violence just as the gangs do; only it is diverted into a religious project. He did his whole sentence. But when he came out, he was involved with people on the edge. There were five arrests last month in Walsall on terrorist offences: two men and three women, accused of helping people go to Syria, and having documents which could be used in a terror conspiracy. One of them was a revert, who had come back to Islam through this man.

'When I came out of prison, I got myself together and went back to Uni. My third attempt! This time it's psychology. I have one year left. I got interested in this, partly as a result of observing what turns people into the path of extremes – the other fork in the road from that which I had taken. Attribution theory explains a lot – these people blame all injustices on the West; and although the West has much to answer for, this is too easy an explanation of the world.

'I think I am lucky to have been born in the UK. I love the open-mindedness. A young Muslim can develop a hybrid mentality, taking from both the West and the Muslim world. Some condemn Western culture as materialistic – its media, music and consumption – and say we have lost Eastern spirituality. They believe we have lost touch with our heritage and all we care about is whether our pockets and bellies are full, a selfish individualism.

'The pressure on people is to conform. This is the secret of gangs and also of intolerant religious groups. The self is de-individualised and lost in the anonymity of belonging. A lot of young Muslims believe there is no right way of making money fast. They feel left out of it. "They fuck with us, let us fuck with them." The rhetoric of the radicals is that the West is fucking Muslims, so why not milk the system here to fund people who are "freedom fighters". The kids in Syria and Palestine need bullets; so use the system, get money in any way you can and send it to them. As a British citizen you cannot enlist in a foreign army. So you help secretly.

'Young Muslims feel cornered. All they can do is punch their way out – rob cars, take them to a garage, get them dismantled and rebuilt, then sell them on and use the money any way you think fit. The story goes that the US and UK were the originators of terrorism. The US destroyed the indigenous population of North America, just as the Aborigines were decimated in Australia, while Britain spread famine and subjugated people all over Africa and Asia.

'There is also a narrative of ungratefulness that can be tapped into: immigrants came here and worked hard, in textiles, the health service, transport, because the British didn't want to do those jobs. The British have lost the work ethic. They are now scroungers and whiners. There is a whole story that we – immigrants in general, but Muslims in particular – have been screwed. They think "I'm here now because my grandfather came here to do work nobody else wanted." They feel pissed off, because their families contributed to society, but they are still not seen as British. If you are told often enough you do not belong, you'll believe it, and look to belong somewhere else.'

Arif says that when his father passed away he felt shame. 'He used to say "We broke our backs to educate you." I wanted to show him that I had heard what he said, even though he was dead. When I came out of prison I got married. My daughter was born just after my father died. I understand now what it means to be a father. My daughter is three. Her mother and

I have split up now; we are on good terms, and we share the care of her.

'From a gang to Islam – it is like a vocational move. The groups that radicalise young people work within certain mosques, but they are also active in prisons and in universities. Nobody seems to care very much about it. The guy in prison came across "the brothers" in this way, and they introduced him to their ideas.

'My own personal morality would not allow me to get involved in such schemes. That is no way to do things. I grew up in England and see the value of much in this society. When I look at Islam, I think of Sufism, which knows nothing of borders. Sufis teach that when you fall in love, you learn that each and every creature on earth is created by God; and for the sake of that, you have to love all living creatures, animals, birds, insects, as well as human beings; and that teaching forbids me to follow the preachers of hatred. There is nothing in Islam that supports what these people are telling the world. I would not say that if the Caliphate existed – not the caricature that calls itself a caliphate now – I would not be on its side. But how can ISIS be a caliphate, when it sets Sunni against Shia? How can they hate Jews? At the time of the caliphs, they all lived side by side.

'There is a story of Ali, son-in-law of the Prophet, PBUH, who became leader of the Shia. He was on the battlefield, and was about to kill an enemy for the sake of his religion and his land. As he raised his sword to bring it down upon him, the enemy spat in his face. And Ali looked at him, and left him. He could not kill him, because if he had done so, it would have been in personal anger, and not for the sake of the high ideals he held.

'I always felt a gap in my life, a void I had to fill. Drugs, alcohol and women were substitutes. I was never very close to my siblings. My friends were my brothers and sisters, and that was where I thought I belonged. I was cool with it, but it did not satisfy the inner craving, the emptiness inside.

'I write lyrics, which are my poetry. I love rap music, and I accompany myself on the ukulele. I love it. I am not George Formby.'

Arif takes out the ukulele and plays as he sings, or chants or raps one of his poems. It is very powerful; linguistically inventive, full of pain and pathos. For Arif, creativity and artistic self-expression occupy the places which others fill with hedonism or religion. There is, he says, no reason why others should not follow a similar path: it is simply that this way is occluded by the clamour of materialism and the drama of religious fervour.

'Those at the forefront of anti-radicalism should be Muslims. The only time you hear Muslims speak in the media is to say "We are not like that" in the wake of some atrocity. Muslims are expected to police the wayward among them, and if they don't, they are somehow collectively responsible for the actions of others.

'There is bound to be a backlash against racism and discrimination. You see it in the reports of young girls being groomed in the old industrial areas. The men are giving back what they feel has been dealt to them, but unfortunately, they choose the wrong people. They see these girls nobody cares for, on the streets, runaways, vulnerable, and they think these are fair game for abuse and exploitation. And society, which doesn't give a damn about the girls until they are abused, becomes all solicitude.

'You can become radicalised and give up nothing. It doesn't matter if you rob, cheat, exploit others, since all the money you make goes to the "brothers". It is the old story of the end justifying the means. Of course there are all kinds of Muslims, just as there are all kinds of people in society in general. There is the majority, who just want a quiet life, others who work hard to educate their children and move up; others who recreate in Wolverhampton a version of rural Pakistan; others who scrounge off the system.'

Arif improvises a song, 'Thank my lucky stars I was born in England'. His warmth and humanity have been nourished by the Sufi Circle in the city, and the teachings he has absorbed there. The leader of the group he calls his 'teacher', who has been a significant figure for him. 'This is what ought to be taught. But it isn't. This is the role model for young Muslims that should reach everyone. As it is, you get crime and drugs on the one hand and religious rage on the other, and the crossover between them; and few people want to listen to the message of hope and humanity that is Islam.'

The idea of reform

The idea of 'reform' has a long and honourable tradition in Britain. It suggests the work of individuals and social movements committed to an extension of the franchise throughout the nineteenth century, as well as those dedicated to campaigns for the mitigation of some of the cruelties of early industrialism: the abridgement of hours of labour, protection for women and children, sanitation, the removal of slum housing. Later reformers and radicals introduced a system of 'welfare', which would defend people against the vagaries of the economic cycle and also against the expected vicissitudes of life – sickness, bereavement and incapacity.

The word 'reform' was revived with great fanfare by the Coalition government in 2010, but no longer with reference to the damage inflicted upon humanity by an economic and social system. It now claimed to deal with the baleful effects of the welfare state – paradoxically, the result of earlier 'reforms', which it was eager to dismantle. Such a project was possible, because while only the ghost of industrial manufacture remained in Britain, the structures of welfare, designed to humanise it, were still in place. It was this tottering relic which – like the factories that had long been crushed into ruins of rubble and splintered glass, the crumbling masonry abandoned to buddleia and willowherb – was now ripe for development by the realtors of modernity.

The rhetoric deployed by government echoes and mocks the passion once used to describe the rescue of the poor from the chronic want and insecurity of the first industrial era. People are now to be 'set free', 'liberated', 'released', not from slum conditions and rapacious employers, but from a grim dependency on welfare, from a fatalistic acceptance of 'benefits' due to long-term – even inter-generational – unemployment. Young people are to be saved from 'sitting at home and falling into depression and despair', emancipated from a 'culture' of mendicancy upon the public purse, and led into the perpetual sunshine of free markets.

In this enterprise, David Cameron, George Osborne and Iain Duncan Smith present themselves as liberators of the people. The 'evils' they address include the beliefs that 'it pays not to work', that we live in a 'something for nothing culture', that 'the world owes us a living', and that the welfare state 'creates a culture of entitlement'. The changes they have introduced to the benefit system will help people 'escape the poverty trap and get on in life'. Proud, self-reliant British people are to be released from the bondage of benefits. The heroic tone of the government's proposals suggests an usurpation of the epic project which Labour once conceived in the interest of 'taming' capitalism, curbing its excesses and redressing the imbalance of power between capital and labour; but the new objective is freedom from an oppressive welfare dependency which will be confronted by today's fearless warriors for liberty. George Osborne reiterated the theme in his budget speech of July 2015, when he spoke of 'transforming the lives of those trapped in welfare'; he made it sound, insultingly, like the situation of miners caught by a rockfall in some industrial catastrophe, while he, in one of his conspicuous hi-vis vests, led the rescue party.

The next sequence in this new enfranchisement of the people is a concession that, however benign the intent of earlier legislation to free them from fear and want, it has led to a situation 'which cannot be cured by money', or 'State hand-outs' as they are now known. This is a bold step, coming as it does from those whose ownership, indeed worship, of wealth is remarkable. Their vocabulary of 'wealth-creationism' has a distinctly religious undertone, so that in their version of the world, the 'generation' of wealth has the quality of a founding myth in the history of capitalist accumulation.

The story was elaborated further by Cameron in June 2012. He said 'The truth is we can't throw money at the problems and paper over the cracks. You can give a drug addict more money in benefits, but that is unlikely to help them out of poverty, indeed it could perpetuate their addiction. You can pump more cash into chaotic homes, but if the parents are still neglectful, the kids are still playing truant, they're going to stay poor in the most important senses of the word. So this government is challenging the old narrow view that the key to beating poverty is simply more redistribution.'

No clearer enunciation is possible of the doctrine that the relief of poverty lies in a withdrawal of State bounty from those who have no need of 'safety-nets' (a persistent image suggesting that being poor is somehow analogous to learning circus skills). No more explicit credo could be imagined: while the rich must be encouraged in their mystical quest to create wealth by heaping more treasures upon them, the poor must be set free by the withdrawal of such meagre resources as they have at their command. Thus, claimed Cameron, the causes of poverty will be treated at their source – 'debt, family breakdown, educational failure, addiction'. It cannot be said that the government does not spin a good yarn: they are consummate storytellers, as they rehearse the heroics of capitalism and the threat to it from its ill-wishers and enemies, whether in the form of organised labour or 'do-gooders' – a pejorative term which hints that the hour of the doers of evil has at last sounded.

If the government really believes the symptoms it identifies are 'causes' of poverty, this demonstrates the shallowness of its understanding of society, the very existence of which, in any case, Mrs Thatcher had long ago thrown into doubt. But the triumphant conclusion lay in what comes next: 'The only thing that really beats poverty, long-term, is work.' If they did not actually carve in iron lettering over the entrance to every Jobcentre the words *Work Sets Free*, this was, no doubt a gesture of tactful forbearance in the light of the abuse of that slogan in another context – although a certain sympathy with the idea is never far from the surface of their rhetoric, since 'work' is the principal instrument of emancipation. (This is not, of course, to suggest that the government has anything in common with the Nazis. The Nazi regime used the phrase as a cruel and diversionary flag of convenience. Unlike the originators of this sinister slogan, our present government actually believes in work as an agent of liberation; no matter how demeaning, futile or degrading it may be. This has a long history, dating back at least to the Elizabethan Poor Law, which insisted all able-bodied paupers should be 'set on work'. For half a millennium, privilege has racked its brains in order to find ways of making a profit out of pauperism.

Armed with these ideological revelations, the project was, according to the government in 2015, far from complete. It would require another 'term' (a language of politics borrowed from school) to 'finish the job' (a term of workmanlike efficiency). The people of Britain, persuaded of the nobility of the cause, granted them this extension.

These thrilling stories make a compelling political narrative, one largely uncontested until Jeremy Corbyn became Labour leader in September 2015; an event which, whatever its subsequent fate, at least enlarged debate and gave a voice to views formerly outlawed by the sometime defenders of the people.

The publicity given to 'cuts', 'crackdowns', reducing the size of the State, flushing out cheats and skivers, the punishment of fraud and the abolition of welfare dependency contains a deeper ideological purpose. Simply because it is couched in the practical terms beloved by the pragmatic no-nonsense British, does not mean it is not underpinned by a philosophy as absolute and rigid as any abstraction dreamed up by scorned continental political theorists. This belief derives from the highly fanciful notion that the 'self-regulating market' is actually an emanation of the natural world, and that the 'laws of economics' are laws of nature, which, as faith in the power of the 'invisible hand' suggests, are also God-given. The fact that Divine Providence does not actually appear in this prospectus does not mean it is absent: though always present, it remains rarely visible.

That our worldly arrangements are of a piece with the natural ordering of the universe has many advantages; not the least being that the authority of nature is self-evident and requires no elaboration in the realm of ideology. It does not depend on any religious texts of revelation, or even secular scripture. Its strength lies in its vaporous quality; like an odourless but deadly gas, pervasive but impalpable, it has the power to injure, and even kill, and leave no trace – as the lengthening list of casualties of a misnamed 'benefits system' shows.

In the early nineteenth century, this was known as laissez-faire: a belief that the market, if left alone, would correct and heal itself, as though the economy were a primitive, self-purifying kind of Gaia. The 'science' of political economy has since then been much elaborated, and is now conducted by the qualified celebrants of the rites of money, the shamans of an animistic wealth 'creation'. This cult swiftly became orthodoxy, and has proved remarkably tenacious, despite the efforts of Marx and others to demolish it and replace it with an altogether more overt elaboration of faith; the working out and exhaustion of which we have witnessed in our lifetime, while the imperishable 'laws' of political economy have gone from strength to strength.

The spectre of laissez-faire was never exorcised. It has remained, the ideological ghost in the machine, to haunt the contemporary world. The Right is penetrated by a persistent nostalgia for a time when, it was imagined, a mythic free market reigned supreme. It never did, of course, does not now, and is never likely to. The greatest obstacle to such a condition of market perfection was always the poor, whose demands upon the State – whether because of their need for sustenance, or their troublesome tendency to organise themselves – have been an obstacle to the smooth working of the sublime mechanism, those 'natural' processes of an economy unchecked by human interference.

Now, with the end of industrial manufacture, the Right has seen a new opportunity, a chance to restore the true faith, and permit the free market to regenerate and establish at last the harmonious equilibrium of that state of nature that is the unfettered play of market forces. The ambition of those who today present themselves as 'conservatives' is the creation of the conditions for a shrunken State, *from which the chaos, violence and cruelty of manufacturing industry have been eliminated*. They are visionaries, and their world is one from which even the memory of industrialism has been erased. The post-industrial world they envisage bears a strong resemblance to its pre-industrial forerunner. Will technology play the role of that once occupied by agriculture, its servants inhabiting a counterfeit pastoral landscape, in which fields and farms are replaced by shimmering screens, electronic transmitters and artificial intelligence, from which data are harvested like corn, and information accumulates in the private granaries of the lords of knowledge?

The stories about deficit reduction and living within our means, like the parables of doing the right thing and abiding by the rules, are mere ornaments to decorate the malignancy beneath. Liberating people from the constraints of welfare does not mean quite what it promises. It means abandoning each individual to make her or his own private accommodation with the vast, impersonal forces of globalisation – perhaps the most unequal and unbalanced contract ever drawn up by even the most dedicated notaries of injustice.

The effects of the early stages of this labour of restoration are already clear – a reversion to the moral and material chastisement of the poor. Detestation of the poor has always been part of the armoury of the rehabilitators of laissez-faire: the persistence of the poor over time dents the conviction that free markets, left to themselves, are the bedrock of human liberty. The continuing presence of large numbers of people who, no matter how hard they try, cannot earn enough to support themselves and those who depend on them remains a formidable disconfirmation of claims made for the liberating power of the market.

Today, in a world which flaunts its wealth, the anti-poor ideology has a more malignant inflexion. For if the stupendous plenty of the modern world co-exists with shocking poverty, so the fable runs, this can be only the fault of the poor, who have failed to avail themselves of all the opportunities for self-enrichment set before them and embodied in an inescapable imagery of abundance; and it is this perversity that must be coerced, compelled, first into recognition of error, and then into rectification of conduct.

That such a bold enterprise should be undertaken at the beginning of the twenty-first century, is significant. It is not that the ideology was not freely elaborated in the early industrial period. It was. But greater caution was required at that time, because the poor – and a category appearing once more, believed for a time to have been abolished, that of the labouring poor – constituted a majority of the population. And although the franchise had not yet been extended to them, their capacity for combination, working together, either as organised labour or as a spontaneous mob, inhibited a too exuberant repression of the poor as the nineteenth century advanced. In the early nineteenth century, of course, before the nature of the new industrial society was fully understood, governments were less squeamish about ordering the military to cut down protesters with sword and sabre, putting down riots with violence, hanging 'ringleaders' and transporting dissenters, demagogues and other ideological criminals to penal colonies.

Ruling elites soon learned a better way: the extension of the franchise to more and more of those who 'had a stake in society', and the provision of that 'stake' to increasing numbers of people. With time, this has had the effect of reducing the poor to minority status; a development which has far-reaching implications. The spectre, transmitted through time, of sturdy rogues and beggars cozening honest citizens out of 'broken meats' and charitable pence, vagabonds and cut-throats haunting the turnpike, idle labourers lolling under hedges munching an onion with one hand, while the other roamed freely under the skirts of wanton trollops, who wanted nothing more than to bear bastard children, since the parish would be sure to find them, had been dealt with by the Poor Law Reform Act of 1834, that uncanny precursor of today's 'reforms'. But its baleful effects were undone by a mixture of popular organisation of the labouring poor (or working class as they came to be known) and the conscience of the high noon of Victorian piety: a double movement, which developed and extended itself, a precursor of the more humanitarian attitudes that culminated much later in the establishment of the welfare state, in the penitent hour after the bones and ashes of the Second World War.

While a majority remained poor, governments were always constrained by the potential power of what E. P. Thompson called the 'revolutionary crowd', which had self-consciously created itself out of the earlier 'mob'. But today, nothing is easier than to marshal punitive majorities against the poor; a process assisted by the fact that those who have no dealings with the welfare system do not understand the vindictiveness of which it is now capable in the hands of those who wield it like a weapon. Indeed, the relationship between the 'beneficiaries' – if that is what they still are – of welfare and the people who do not fall under its flinty provision, is hidden from view, appearing only in an occasional TV exposé or a rare newspaper account of what poor people must expect to endure in the interests of 'deficit reduction', that most flimsy of screens for secular revenge on those who remained untouchable as long as they formed a refractory, and possibly mutinous, multitude in the industrial towns and cities of the country.

Today's 'new poor law', although not officially designated as such, owes much to its early nineteenth-century predecessor. The law of less eligibility enshrined in the Poor Law Amendment Act of 1834 – which declared that the worst-paid labourer outside the workhouse should be better off than the most comfortable inmate within the chill embrace of its walls – is resuscitated in the assertion that work, any work, all work, no matter how humiliating or ill-paid, must offer a better life than an existence on welfare. It should not surprise us that the government does not propose the reconstruction of workhouses up and down the land. There is no need: impoverished estates, crumbling privately rented tenements, run-down properties in town centres and on exurban settlements ensure an experience that has no need of formal institutions for the enforcement of these wholesome doctrines.

Positive results are claimed for this experiment with the recipients of welfare, although, as with any potent 'medicine' (another favourite metaphor of Conservative politicians), side-effects are always observable. Some of these may not have been intentional, but remedies have rarely succeeded in curing the ills for which they have been prescribed by those modern-day practitioners of alchemy, the doctors of economic divinity; a fact which leads only to the devising of even more gruelling conditions for the unfortunate petitioners before the benefits system. In 2014, the Department for Work and Pensions suggested that a monetary levy could be raised from people who appealed against its decisions: of the 900,000 cases of benefits stopped between 2013 and 2014, 58 per cent were overturned on appeal (*Guardian*, 20 February 2014).

People with disability

During the 1980s, when much manufacturing industry was closing down in Britain, unemployment was high. It became expedient for the then Thatcher government to conceal the true extent of worklessness. This was achieved, in part, by registering many people as sick or disabled; a category which removed people from the workplace without transferring them to the already swollen ranks of the unemployed. Many were indeed victims of stress, depression and anxiety; or older workers, exhausted or physically damaged by a lifetime of heavy manual labour. The criteria were not applied with great severity, since the principal function of the statistics was to hide the catastrophic loss of industrial employment in those years.

Rectifying this became part of the project of the Coalition government from 2010 to 2015, confirmed by the subsequent Conservative administration. Many people psychically and emotionally wounded by the loss of their life's work, and the diminishing of all they had done and contributed to the wealth of Britain (the story of the miners' strike and its defeat speaks for itself), are, of course, now well beyond retirement age. But it has been the government's objective to 'tighten up' or 'crack down' on those who have, allegedly, or in fact, abused the system, since this forms part of their rhetoric of emancipation: people with disability, for instance, do not wish to remain 'stuck on benefit' for an indefinite period. It is true that most people want to contribute some useful skill or ability to society; the more so, since the experience of people with disability often gives them insights and understanding which others do not possess.

There is everything to be said for facilitating the passage of people with disability into the labour force according to their capacity. But this becomes oppressive when the priority is a lowering of numbers receiving benefit, putting pressure on people who are vulnerable, lack confidence, or are too weak or frightened to compete in the labour market. 'Incentives' to get people into work have been outsourced to private profit-making entities, whose very existence depends upon their 'success' in cajoling or threatening people into employment, many of whom cannot perform the labour which they have been passed as fit for by Work Capability Assessments. These are crude and mechanistic judgements, and take little account of the situation of those they judge. This has also been supported by government rhetoric about people feigning disability in order to avoid doing a fair day's work. It is a short step from this – a campaign, noisily and maliciously pursued by the press, much of which is now apparently an elective arm of the government information service – to a belief that the disabled in general fall into the category of idlers and scroungers, to be placed alongside crooked characters uncovered by the media who are found to be refereeing football matches or taking part in gymnastics displays while in receipt of benefits for back pain or injuries sustained in a car accident.

Hate crimes against people with disability have reached record levels. According to the Crime Survey of England and Wales in 2012/13, 62,000 disabled people said they had been victims, although less than 2,000 of these had been recorded by the police, of which only about a quarter resulted in conviction. A much wider incidence of low-level harassment and discrimination was reported, while it was estimated that the phasing out of Disability Living Allowance would remove the benefits altogether of well over half a million people.

It is one of the great ironies that a new Conservative administration should want to undo the mischief of an older one, now that the earlier act of deception has served its purpose; and beneath the rhetoric of 'emancipation' lies a darker story of coercion and punishment. It requires very little in the curiously understated semaphore of public communication in Britain to hint at the exclusion or outlawry of one group or another; and people with disability have often found themselves, to their astonishment, classed under the expanding category of the 'undeserving' in society.

In any case, astute and adaptable, the government has discovered more sophisticated ways of concealing the true extent of unemployment and underemployment; this time by encouraging an upsurge in 'self-employment', much of it sham or ineffective, but enough to take perhaps hundreds of thousands of people off the unemployment total. And if they are not claiming 'benefits', many qualify for in-work tax credits, and are, in effect, subsidised by the taxpayer, that heroic figure of the Right, burning with resentment at the waste of his (the taxpayer is a male icon) money on the extravagant and undeserving, or on causes far from his heart.

Perhaps it is partly in reaction against the policy of the Thatcher years, which the Conservatives now perceive as having been too 'lenient' on disability, that this group now seems to have been singled out for particular punishment. In October 2014, Lord Freud, Welfare Reform Minister, incautiously expressed the view that there is a group in society who are 'not worth the full wage', and might be paid as little as £2 an hour. His giving voice to this insight threw some doubt on the concept of the 'compassionate Conservatism' ostensibly espoused by Cameron.

The disability charity Scope, together with Demos, have published research showing that by 2017/18, 3.7 million people with disability, both those in work and those not working, will lose £28 billion in benefits. A combination of cuts and restrictions to Employment and Support Allowance, the replacement of Disability Living Allowance with Personal Independence Payments, the capping of rises to benefits and tax credits, along with local authority reduction or abolition of council tax exemptions, will further remove those already on the margin of society from full participation. The DWP argues that the 'targeting' of benefits will be more efficient; an expression which makes benefits sound like a weapons system rather than an arm of the welfare state (see www.demos.co.uk/ press_releases/destinationunknownapril2013).

In the budget of July 2015, further 'savings' in this area were foreshadowed. The Employment and Support Allowance has been allocated to two distinct groups: those incapable of working for the foreseeable future (the Support Group); and those for whom future work is possible (the Work-Related Activity Group). The ESA for the latter group is to be reduced in April 2017 to the equivalent of Jobseeker's Allowance, which will cut their benefit by about 30 per cent.

Undermining the security of people with disability creates more problems than it solves, in terms of emotional and psychiatric disturbance, anxiety and depression. Iain Duncan Smith persistently couches his intentions in the most benign terms. He reverts to the assertion that 'work is good for your health'. It is true that most people, including those with disability, want to contribute to the work of society; it is of a piece with the rhetoric about 'liberating' people. But we have seen how compulsion is used. When Duncan Smith insists that support is there 'for the most vulnerable people in society', he follows it with a distinct menace: 'We must not stop there. We need to be relentless in our efforts to get more people into work and off welfare.' The word 'relentless' quite properly strikes a chill into many people with disability; the more so since the stigma of being a 'skiver' hovers over all claimants, and some employers are not necessarily exempt from prejudice against those who suffer from physical or mental disability. Employers may 'give' people work, but this does not turn them into charities.

Amanda

Amanda has been blamed by people in her neighbourhood for her failure to work, as indeed was her husband, who died shortly before I met her.

Amanda, in her late thirties, lives in a small bungalow. The porch is decorated with coloured plastic flowers, the interior homely and cluttered. On the mantelpiece is a picture of Desmond, her husband, who died in March 2014, and an enlarged wedding photograph, taken 14 years earlier. The wallpaper has a motif of bright red poppies; Desmond decorated the room shortly before he died.

This was the only house I visited in November where the heating was on. Amanda's condition requires warmth, since one of its symptoms is low body temperature.

Amanda is still in mourning for her husband, and this coloured our conversation. Desmond's diabetes led to pancreatitis and early death.

'He went into hospital for what was to have been a routine treatment. We said "I love you" to each other before I left. Next day, I had a call to say he had an infection and was in intensive care. I went down to the hospital at once. They were sorry, but he needed an operation. I was given a consent form to sign. If I didn't sign it, he would die. They expected him to make a full recovery. He had septicaemia.

'The next day, he did not wake up. He had had a fit; and, starved of oxygen for four minutes, he had also been brain-damaged. Four days later, the oxygen support was turned off and he died. The doctor who told me he had died could not speak English, and we had to have an interpreter in the room.

'I have lived those four days again and again ever since. We were all in all to each other. We looked after each other and he was devoted to me. He was 55. He had worked as a porter for the NHS for 15 years; then at a hydraulics company where he became a manager. He gave that up to become my carer in 2000.

'He is here with me all the time. I speak to him. I say to the neighbours "If you hear me talking, don't think I've gone mad. I'm only talking to Desmond."

'My sister is now my carer, but she doesn't receive anything for it, because she is just above the income limit, and she doesn't actually live with me. She is close by. She works for an insurance company, and her husband manages a leisure centre, so, with the family, they are always busy. I have to have someone keep watch on me, because I am on controlled drugs.'

Amanda has neurofibromatosis, which causes an inflammation of the nervous system. Joseph Merrick, known as the Elephant Man, suffered from a version of this. His deformities were external, whereas Amanda's are internal. The condition affects about one person in 3,000. Joseph Merrick was born in Leicester in 1862; rejected by his stepmother and father after the death of his mother, he entered the workhouse in Leicester at the age of 17. He was subsequently exhibited all over the country by a showman, and died in 1890, probably because the weight of his head was greater than his body could bear.

Amanda has suffered a broken back and tumours inside her body. These have to be removed. One tumour at the base of her spine weighed two and a half pounds. Amanda also has soft bones – different from brittle bones, but they are still fragile. One night she felt uncomfortable and in the morning discovered she had fractured ribs. Amanda does not know what it means to be free of pain. But because it is not immediately visible, people are less sympathetic than they might be.

In spite of her disabilities, Amanda radiates warmth and concern for others. Generous of spirit, she says that her own pain has given her insight into the sufferings of other people, even if theirs are quite different from her own. 'If I came back into the world again, I would still choose to come as myself.' Her parents have been 'wonderful'. Her father was a bus conductor on West Midlands buses, but retired early with cerebral ataxia. Her mother worked at Tesco's for 18 years. She had an accident at work: she slipped on some liquid spilt on the floor. She did eventually get compensation.

Amanda's condition is hereditary. Her mother is affected, but not her sister. Her grandmother had the same condition. Amanda first underwent surgery when she was three. The doctors knew then what was wrong, but they didn't tell her family until she was 11.

'I live on Employment and Support Allowance. While Desmond was alive, we got £245 a fortnight. Now I get £178. I have £90 a month from my husband's pension, and Disability Living Allowance of £172. The rent is paid directly to the landlord. Electricity is expensive – £80 a month – because I can't be cold. When all the bills are paid, I don't lead a life of luxury. I once rang the Jobcentre when my money had run out, and I asked the woman "What shall I live on?" She said "beans on toast" and put the phone down. I have to pay the bedroom tax, £14 a week. The bedroom is not even half a room. I keep my electric wheelchair there. I got in touch with my MP, David Winnick. He was disgusted. There is apparently no discretionary payment for disabled people. My case is going to tribunal next month. Fortunately, my parents make me a small monthly payment for the tax.' The tribunal decided against Amanda, and she is still paying.

'I have a car. That is, literally, my lifeline. We bought it just before Desmond died. He never got to drive it. He used a wheelchair. He was diagnosed with genetic diabetes in his forties. He needed insulin. They put him on some tablets which caused the pancreatitis. That can also be a result of drinking alcohol, but he was teetotal. They changed the tablets when it was found out they were damaging him, but it was too late.

'I take Fentanyl, a painkiller, 75 milligrams a day. It is an opiate, used as an anaesthetic in surgery. I also take 21 other painkillers during the day, which dull the pain but do not remove it.

'I don't get bored, but naturally, I am still grieving. I keep occupied. I make cards – Christmas cards, birthday cards, sympathy cards, anniversaries of all kinds. I also love baking – birthday cakes, fruit cakes, cupcakes. I made a cake for the 16th birthday of my best friend's daughter. I couldn't take money for it. I have never taken anything from anyone. I would love to be able to work. I had a job, voluntary classroom assistant in a school for children with special needs. I had to stop, because it was exhausting and left me the following day unable to do anything. Of course you get judged. Although I have to use a crutch to walk, I've been called lazy, a bitch. People have called us "spongers".'

In official buildings in the city – libraries, council offices, housing associations – there are signs asking people to report Disability Hate Crimes. Many people with disability say that this is a direct result of the government onslaught against 'welfare cheats'. Some people cited the character in the TV series Little Britain, a wheelchair-bound man who, when his carer is not looking, leaps up and performs feats of intense activity. Although intended as a comic sketch, it has had a wide resonance, and, to some, confirms the idea that all people in wheelchairs are sham.

'Even those who should know better are prejudiced. Desmond was married before. His son was very unsympathetic. He said we simply wouldn't get off our backsides. He lives in Devon with his partner. I don't see them. Desmond's first marriage broke down. I met him soon after. We met in Malta, a holiday romance. Five months later, we were engaged. His mother moved up here in 2012, so we could take care of her. It was a mistake, because away from her familiar background, everything was wrong. I did all I could for her, but it was not a happy relationship.

'After Desmond died, she went back to Devon. She wanted to take Desmond's ashes with her. It isn't seemly to fight over a loved one's remains. She said to me once "You're the best thing that ever happened to my son. But not to me."

'We had good years while it lasted. He is here with me. All the time. He used to say to me "I'll never leave you." And he hasn't left me. I can't say I believe in God. If there is a God, why would he allow all the pain, the suffering there is in the world? A friend died of cancer a few months ago. She was 36. My father is an atheist. I wouldn't go that far, because I think there is something beyond this life, even if we don't know what it is.

'I get a lot of help from people: my parents, my sister, and the people next door are wonderful neighbours. I generally have one meal a day. I go to Sainsbury's before they close, because you can get cheap deals on food on its sell-by date. In the evening, when I've taken my medication, I close the door and get into my pyjamas.

'I have a very unusual dog, a trained diabetic dog. She is with my father now.' Amanda shows me a picture of the dog, called Princess. 'A diabetic dog can tell when a patient is going to have hypoglycaemia, when blood sugar drops below 4.0. They have to be trained for eight weeks. You train the dog by putting her on the patient's lap. She can lick and smell the skin, until the dog understands the indications when a hypoglycaemic state is approaching. She understands. We had her for my husband, and she would come and tell me if anything untoward was due to happen. She is a little angel. She won't eat dog food, so I have to prepare special food for her.'

Amanda and Desmond couldn't have children. They had been approved as adoptive parents, and were waiting for a child. Amanda thought the social workers didn't like them. She suspects somebody had written to Social Services to say they would be unfit parents. 'Or perhaps they thought we weren't robust enough to look after a child. Anyway, it never happened. Actually it was a blessing, because this was only two years ago.

'I do get help. EDF [Électricité de France] has a charity called Warm Front, which makes an allowance for heating to the elderly and disabled. I get £140 a year discount on my electricity. But most letters are demands for money. I was two weeks late paying the bedroom tax, and I got a phone call asking "Where is it?" They never contact you when they owe you something.

'I'm afraid of the Personal Independence Payment. I'm frightened they will take my car. I would be utterly lost. If there are two disabled people living together, they can be each other's carer. Every time I look at TV, I'm afraid of what the government is going to do next. I wrote to David Cameron – he, having had a disabled child, ought to understand how it is for people.

'I get angry when people accuse me of being a cheat. I know there are people who sit on their backside when they are capable of working. My mother's next-door neighbour has nine children, between the ages of 19 and three. She has never worked.'

During my time in the West Midlands, many people on benefit – often disabled or severely disadvantaged in some way – expressed their resentment at the vilification of people like themselves. But in order to vindicate their own position, it seems, many have to contrast their situation, and the falsehoods attributed to it, with that of the *truly* undeserving. There is an extensive folklore about people living off the State. A common story at the end of 2014 was of a woman 'flown from Africa' to have a Caesarean birth on the National Health Service, simply because she had a visa to enter Britain. The cost was £10,000. People had heard of 'asylum seekers' arriving at the council offices and being given priority accommodation over people who have lived here all their lives. 'They can't do enough for foreigners, while our own people are second-class citizens' was a recurring refrain.

Such stories should be taken seriously, since they are metaphors for feelings of injustice. To engage with them in order to refute or deny them is vain work. They are illustrative but deeply-felt moral tales; the outer shell of a profound wound to the sensibility of people who have never been consulted about anything that concerns their sense of who they are, and yet are expected obediently to play a democratic game which seems to affect them only minimally. Such stories are incantations hurled at an indifferent Authority, which protects injustice and inequality and reinforces people's sense of powerlessness. Here are the roots of UKIP, who are speaking to a sense of loss and disregard, to Labour's 'lost people', the unrepresented and disfranchised, exiles of democracy. This has all been 'pioneered' in the USA, where large tracts of society are derelict, and the freedom to be as poor as one chooses has been elevated into the highest liberty. But the USA is another place; it has space and an openness unavailable in a cramped island weighed down by the historic freight of a violent industrialism and its subsequent unravelling.

Belfort: survival

One question is asked rhetorically, since those who pose it rarely expect an answer: Is life not attended by sufficient grief and pain without it being exacerbated by the actions of our fellow-humans, especially those in power; and what purpose is served by intensifying our suffering *as a matter of principle* by government? Although most people with disability do not claim heroic status, the efforts required of them for survival can only make us wonder at the stoicism and endurance with which many face the social disadvantage which adds to existential afflictions that must be lived with.

Belfort has spent much of his life negotiating a pathway through the dual menace of prejudice and pity, social and personal. Born in Birmingham in 1980, his family moved to Wolverhampton in 1991. There were seven children, and Belfort's disability meant he needed a room to himself. 'Until then, I shared a room with my brother, and had to be carried up and down stairs. It was unsatisfactory. So when a six-bedroom house became vacant here, we couldn't turn it down.

'My father was from Jamaica, my mother from Birmingham. At birth, I was apparently all right for a week, but then I had some kind of fit, and the oxygen failed to get to the brain. I was diagnosed with cerebral palsy. The doctor told my parents "He won't be able to talk or do anything." That became a determining factor in my upbringing. My mother must have thought "Give him a life, not necessarily a good life, but the best we can do." She never used to kiss me. I think they felt that I was not going to last very long, so they didn't want to get too attached. One day, as my auntie was leaving the house, she kissed me. My mother said "Why don't you let me kiss you?" I said "I don't stop you." It was she who was holding back. I would never ask her if that was because of what the doctor said, but it must have been.

'I went to a school for children with disabilities, and whatever I got there, it was not an education. We were taught to a very limited level, because it was assumed we would never amount to anything. I couldn't read when I left school. I looked at the M of McDonald's, and associated the shape of the arch with the restaurant. At school, I felt I was deliberately kept back. They did the same material over and over again. If I said "I learned that last year", they would say I was a rebel.'

Belfort was transferred to an ordinary school, but couldn't cope, because he was still illiterate. At 15, heartbroken, he was returned to the special school. He couldn't even tell the time. Little was expected of children whose mental capacity was – wrongly – assumed to be impaired. Belfort was never really tested: no one tried to discover what he was capable of. Accustomed to being carried everywhere, he says he was very passive. Only when he was 16 did he think he ought to take control of his life.

'I found the continuous noise and music of my brothers and sisters overwhelming. I knew the schooling I had was rubbish, and I wanted to learn. I decided to go to college in Nottingham [Portland College for people with disabilities]. I didn't tell anyone I had applied. I went for an assessment and I liked it. There was a one-week course, called The Sky's the Limit, which showed how the college worked. It also gave me a chance to experience life away from the family. I got in. I was nervous about telling them. I said to my father "By the way, I'm going to college." They didn't want to sign the consent form, because if I left home, my benefits would stop. Somebody from the college gave a presentation at the school. He recognised me and said "Where is your application form?" "My mother and father don't want me to go."

In the end, they agreed. I think they felt I would never be able to cope. I was there three years and grew more and more independent. I learned more in college than I did all the years at school. In fact, the problem came when I went back home. My family were busy and had no time to take me around. I wanted to move to Nottingham, but there was no accommodation. I was very depressed, because it meant a return to dependency and immobility.'

Belfort remained at home for four years. He attended a Day Centre, and eventually observed that some people were not going back to the family home at night, since they lived in a residential hostel. Belfort decided he, too, would like his own accommodation. He moved into Meadowsweet House, designed specifically for people with disability.

'The trouble was, the carers did everything for you. I told them not to, it made you even more dependent. I wanted to learn to cook and clean for myself, to organise my own affairs. I was becoming lazy, and worse, less capable.

'I wanted to move out. The story everywhere was of long waiting lists. I was registered with a housing association, but they took for ever to process my application. To them, I was already in a secure living place. I wrote to the council, complaining about the wait. They sent someone to Meadowsweet House, who asked how anybody dared to complain on my behalf.

They thought I was incapable of expressing my own protest. I'm listening to this man shouting at the carer, and then I say "And how dare you assume I am not competent to write my own letter of complaint?" Within two days they had given me priority on the waiting list, and within six weeks I got the flat where I've lived for six years. It had to be adapted – I needed a hoist, the doorknobs had to be lowered so I could reach them from my wheelchair.'

It is one thing for government ministers to declare they are going to free people from 'dependency', when their motives are rarely uninfluenced by a concern for 'the public purse', but quite another when individuals themselves declare their own independence. This may be a matter of public policy, but it must be at the pace and to the degree determined by the individuals concerned. That requires far more consultation and commitment to the autonomy and self-respect of the people themselves. This would, of course, require more intensive training, a different kind of consciousness from that with which most employees of private businesses or government agencies approach the issues involved. Neither the profit motive nor bureaucratic expediency offers much chance of a humane response. If Belfort has triumphed, it is in spite of those whose function it is to care for him.

'A carer comes twice a day, in the morning and at night. They stay half an hour each time. When I began to live alone, I was surprised at how independent I was. When everything is done for you, you don't test yourself, you do not know what you are capable of. I have always been underestimated. If anybody says anything to me now, if anybody shows disrespect for my disability, I'll say something back. I never used to. But now, I won't let them walk away, because I am left wishing I had spoken up.

'I wouldn't say I've had a hard life. The problem is the way other people have thought about me. If I'm in a group of able-bodied people, they'll do everything but look at me and talk to me. I have to be assertive. I make people laugh, and when they see I can have a joke they are surprised. I love to laugh. I can be serious, but I don't want people to think I'm miserable. Until I was 16 I never spoke up for myself. I was passive, I thought that was normal. With my brothers, and especially my cousins, I got left out. Despite being one of the oldest in the family, I was treated like a younger brother. I remained dependent.

'My family are still close. We talk on the phone, although I don't see them very often. My father works making spare parts for washing machines. My mother used to manage the YMCA, helping homeless people find a place to live. They went back to Birmingham.

'Some time ago, I was taken to a Jobcentre, to see what kind of work I might be able to do. I said "I have been disabled from birth, and it can only get worse with time. Put me down for as many jobs as you like. What do you suggest?" If they take me up again I shall call it harassment and take them to court.

'I don't care how people see me. The most annoying thing is when people talk on my behalf, as though I can't speak for myself. I try to live at a distance. I keep bad news out of my head. I don't read papers or see the news. If I see a horror movie, I go to bed and have apocalyptic dreams. I keep away from negative things.

'It isn't that I wouldn't work. I'd love to teach. I could teach life skills to people with disability; teach people how to get along, be co-operative instead of competitive.

'I've had a number of relationships. The further away people are, the better the relationship. I don't have a girlfriend at the moment. I could say I was lonely. I get bored easily, and I do sabotage myself. I'm always thinking of how a relationship will end, even at the beginning. On the other hand, I have never dumped a girl. I would never be the one to finish a relationship. I am the one who gets dumped.

'Being self-reliant isolates you to some extent. A lot of people see only the wheelchair. I look at them looking at the wheelchair, and I can tell immediately whether or not we are going to move beyond that. I don't use my disability. I don't like people staring at me. I am not here to be looked at. I don't mind when children come and talk, that's different. But I hate prejudice. Ignorance is the worst disability of all, and it's invisible.'

Lorraine: in the benefits labyrinth

Families with children have been among the hardest hit, especially those affected by the 'benefit cap'. This was introduced in 2013, and set at £26,000 a year. The government claimed it was morally indefensible for anyone not working to receive in benefits a sum greater than the average wage. This was disingenuous, for it took no account of the benefits available to people in work. If the limit were based upon average income, and not average earnings, it would be set at about £31,500. The claim that the existing system rewards 'worklessness' was simply untrue; but as political rhetoric it was effective and commanded much public support. The cap has subsequently been reduced to £23,000 in London and £20,000 outside the capital.

How much money will be saved by this ideologically driven policy is unknown. It may well encourage families to separate – contrary to the intention of Iain Duncan Smith, whose reverence for families is well known. A family with six children would be better off living separately and sharing the children between two households – potentially receiving £1,000 a week between them rather than the cap of £500.

The cap applies independently of the number in the family, and breaks the crucial connection between need and benefits. There is also an element of 'deterrence' in the policy, designed to discourage people from having large families. The government announced that from April 2017 families with more than two children will not receive tax credits or housing benefit for their third child or any subsequent children. This will not affect the 870,000 families with three or more children presently claiming tax credits, nor the basic child benefit. It is part of a coercive policy designed to 'change behaviour'; a curiously meddlesome aspect of a government that claims to promote freedom from State interference, but shows itself to be pettily interventionist wherever this is politically expedient.

If this policy is aimed at the unborn, there is already a considerable armoury available to train on those already born, whose income has dwindled at the very moment they need it most. I am reminded of a family I met in the north of England some years ago. The couple had seven children. The father heard his neighbour complain about families with 'too many children'. He called the children into the garden and lined them up. 'Now', he challenged the neighbour, 'you tell me which ones I should not have had.'

On a November afternoon at four o'clock it is almost dark. The street of former council houses is a mixture of neat gardens, with winter pansies and red cyclamen, and neglect – flags of St George, a warning of dangerous dogs, concrete yards littered with sodden furniture, rusty metal, food wrappings blown about by the wind. In the environment may be read the morale of those who live here: external neglect reflects unhappiness or chaos within. Many of these are the objects of the government's 'troubled families' programme, for which it claims 'success in turning lives around'; as though these lives were unwieldy vehicles that required nothing more than an instructor with advanced driving skills.

In *Lorraine*'s house, Christmas decorations are already in place. It is November 17th. Streamers from the central light fitting are attached to the walls, while a Christmas tree that almost reaches the ceiling is swathed in coloured paper garlands, so the green is virtually invisible. Large Santa socks are pinned to the wall. Lorraine says with resignation, 'I'll have to take another loan for Christmas.'

It is impossible to exaggerate the importance of Christmas to poor families. On the estate, there are many festive trees with multi-coloured lights. Anticipation starts early. If Christmas is a symbolic festival here, this is because it has carried into a secular world something of the sacredness of childhood, only distantly connected with its Christian origins. The occasion has shed its direct association with religion and taken on a new one: whether a celebration of giving or spending, it exercises a compulsion over parents as no other event in the year does. People say 'I have to give my children the best Christmas I can';

'I'll do anything to see they don't go without at Christmas'; 'I will steal if I have to for Christmas.'

The children are in their dressing-gowns, well-worn candlewick wraps, because the family cannot afford heating. All six children – aged from four to 13 – are friendly and smiling. The first thing you feel as you enter this house is that, whatever the material deficiencies, there is no shortage of love. Lorraine is a defiant defender of her children, without regard for economic and social consequences. Shannon, the youngest, is eating bread and butter while waiting for her tea. Today's menu is chips and gravy; but all have had a school meal at mid-day. Lorraine says 'I can't give them nutritious food. They eat junk. That's all we can afford.'

The house had previously been three flats, but the housing association converted it to single occupancy, since there are few houses big enough in the city for large families.

'Before we moved in, somebody broke into the property and took all the copper piping and the radiators; so technically we were squatting. We had to move out of the place where we were before. When we first came, the full rent was paid, but with the benefit cap, our income went down, because with six children we were over the £500 a week limit. I signed for accommodation for eight people; but now I'm also being charged for the bedroom tax, because they think the children should share rooms.'

Vince, Lorraine's husband, is on Employment and Support Allowance, which replaced incapacity benefit. He became so ill with worry about money and debt he tried to take his own life. He cannot be left on his own. While we talk, he sits with the children in the kitchen.

Lorraine is hopelessly in debt. It is impossible to disentangle the family's finances. 'I was in court for non-payment of rent, to which I'm supposed to contribute £114.50 a week, out of a total income of £416. I had arrears of £2,800. They want an extra £109 a month to bring it down. There is help for people, but nobody tells you – you have to find out for yourself. I managed to get school uniforms for the children, because if you are on free meals you are entitled to them.

'I had to go to court for payment of a TV licence. They fined me £500, and I pay £7 a week, but that is for last year. You're running behind all the time, because I still haven't paid this year. I've got a £900 loan from Provident. I owe more than £600 on electricity, and I'm paying through the meter: every time I put money on the card, I have to pay an extra £4.

'It grieves me that the children don't have what others take for granted. My benefits have been sanctioned: first time it's four weeks, then three months, and after that it can be three years. If you don't get Jobseeker's Allowance or Income Support, they can stop your tax credit money. If you are sanctioned you don't get housing benefit. You keep only your child benefit and child tax credit, because they can't make your children suffer, although they suffer all the time. With the benefit cap I was only 63 pence over the limit, but you become liable for a contribution towards rent and council tax. All that is supposed to come out of your reduced income.'

The children are also made to feel shame in other ways. The older girls are called 'scrubbers' at school. The eldest is studying fashion and design. The school wants £29 for her to go on a trip as part of her studies. Lorraine looks at the letter from the school 'Where will I find the money for that? Yet if I don't, I'm letting her down.'

Lorraine knows the government says that if people's incomes are reduced, they will find a job to make it up. 'There are no jobs. They said if we went to work, we'd get our wages and child benefit, but the child tax credits would go down, so we would wind up in the same position, or even worse. In any case, I can't leave Vince, and what will the four-year-old do? My children are 13, 12, 11, 9, 8 and 4. They are talking of reducing child tax credits to a maximum for two children. If that is to discourage people from having kids, what are they going to do with those already here?'

Lorraine is well aware that the way they live is 'terrible. We live day to day. My husband is under psychiatric care. All we have is family. Vince's sister and her daughter live nearby. My mother is down the road, and my younger sister lives with her. We are friends with the people next door. If I have nothing, I sometimes go and ask her for a drop of milk.'

Lorraine and Vince were married in 2014. They had lived together for 15 years, and they wanted something to celebrate in a bleak social world. An event. It was paid for by the family. 'It was low key, but we felt we wanted to express our love for each other.' One of the least commented on aspects of poverty is an inability to mark the important moments in life, the solemnity and significance of love, of survival and still being together.

'I have sold furniture to feed the children.'

In the living room there is a long L-shaped sofa, where all the family can sit together to watch TV, which is fixed high on the wall. Apart from this and the Christmas tree, there is no other furniture. The rest of the house is equally thinly furnished. 'You have to sell everything you've got to pay the housing bill. Since Vince has been on Employment and Support Allowance, the

rent has been reduced to £98 a month. We have five bedrooms;
but with four girls and two boys, they are expected to share, so
with Vince and me in another room, in theory that makes the
spare bedroom for which we are being charged.

'I take responsibility for the household. Although we work
as a team, it falls mainly to me. Vince is on heavy medication.
He won't sit here while we talk about this, because it just
throws him into deep despair. I used to sail through life. It was
easier; but it seems it has been made deliberately harder. I try
to show a good face to the world, but when I'm alone, I cry,
when nobody can see me. I try to lift things up in the family,
but it is an effort sometimes.

'Of course kids don't understand. How could they? They
sometimes blame me for what they can't have. They can't have
mobile phones, tablets, computers – things children expect
these days. I used to worry about money, but do you know
what – in the end, what you haven't got they can't take. I do
a big shop at Lidl every week, spend between £120 and £150
on food. We don't eat fruit. I give them cereal for breakfast,
take two big bottles of milk a day. Three loaves. At tea-time
it's a sandwich or jacket potato. My youngest loves sliced ham
out of a packet. I do sausage or pie with peas and carrots at
weekend; sometimes chips, pie and vegetable.

'The only time I put the heating on is when it snows or gets
really cold. It has become harder in the last few years. I used
to get a free prescription for all of them when they got head
lice: now I have to go to the doctor for each one. It happens at
the school, you can't prevent it. To buy, it costs £15 a bottle.
As a teenager, you don't get a free prescription, because they
are supposed to look after themselves. But it isn't their fault,
whether they are two or 12.

'I had a good childhood. It makes me feel like crap because they are getting less than I had. When Vince took his overdose, he said "I thought you'd be better off without me." That's terrible. What has happened that makes people feel like that? I can't leave him alone. He will have a medical to see if he can get PIP. If he does, all the rent will be paid, and we will be better off. It's come to something when you'd rather be ill than healthy. Last election, I sat here and couldn't believe it when I saw this lot had got in.

'When the children are small, you keep them under your eye. It's when they start to grow up the real worry starts. I think boys are more vulnerable than girls – you see them about here, smoking dope openly. You can't control who they mix with – crime, drugs, taking and driving. If I could pick up this house and move it somewhere else, I would. When they knew where we were going to live, people said "Don't go down there." But you make your home your own.

'You have to be tough. When we first moved in, there were no gates to the front garden. One day a guy parked his van on my garden. I went out and said to him "Take it away or I'll trample all over the roof." He soon backed off. That's how it is. You have to stand up for yourself, because nobody else will.'

Lorraine is 32. She spends nothing on herself. The first time she went to court for debt, she felt shame. But with time, it becomes another ritual. It stops being the terror it was. It no longer intimidates. She says 'You can't stop people being poor, but you can pass laws that make them poorer. That's why poverty *is* a crime, but it isn't poor people that commit it.'

As I left the house, a middle-aged woman and her daughter were calling. Lorraine is at the centre of community networks, which are her lifeline. It is only by the grace of such people that Lorraine keeps the family together; she is grateful to them. The family was exempted from the benefit cap early in 2015, because of the state of Vince's health.

It requires particular courage for Lorraine to confront her debts, look after the children and take care of Vince. There are many women like her.

At the same time, others are asking for their children to be taken into care. In March 2014, there were 68,840 children in care in the UK, an increase of 14 per cent since 2008. In part, this was a response to the notorious Baby P. case in Haringey, but I met several mothers who had voluntarily surrendered their children into care, because they could not cope, or their children were beyond their control. They said 'They will be better off being looked after.' Passing over children to the State is a decision not taken lightly. It sets up a cycle of guilt and remorse, and reinforces a sense of inadequacy.

Jayne Durham

Analysis of the effects of the budget of July 2015 by the Joseph Rowntree Foundation in September 2015 demonstrates that single-parent families are among those most seriously disadvantaged by the changes announced. Julia Unwin, Chief Executive of the Foundation, says 'The budget has transformed the relationship between pay, benefits and work incentives. Lone parents, even working full time, face sharply declining living standards.'

Among them is *Jayne Durham*, a warm, apparently relaxed woman, comfortable with herself, but, underneath, fretting constantly about the two children who remain with her: Brett, two and Jayden, 13 months. The living room in the house is full of toys – plastic cars, engines, coloured bricks, soft toys, animals, plastic guns. It is like an emporium of goods made in China for the children of the world. As we talk, Jayne sits Jayden in her lap. Brett goes to the kitchen and comes back with fruit – bananas and oranges. Jayne breaks a banana and gives half to Jayden. 'They love fruit'. She got ten bananas for 87 pence and a packet of six oranges for 90 pence at Asda. If Jayne is anxious to display her good parenting ability, this is because of the absence of her older children, who are in care.

Jayne is in debt. 'I have a loan of £500, and I'm paying that off at £43 a fortnight.' Her rent arrears come to about £399. 'I have to pay £3.70 a week for 12 weeks, and then they will transfer me to another property. I need a smaller place, because I am being charged bedroom tax at £13.40 a week. It's actually two and a half bedrooms, but they won't allow each child his own room. I joined the Facebook group fighting the bedroom tax. I also owe £1,400 on water bills. It costs £5 a day for electricity in the cold weather – £35 a week. I get £103 in benefit, £33 child benefit and £102 Income Support. Out of that I am also expected to pay £13 a month towards council tax. It is impossible. I always put the children first.'

It was just before the general election of 2015. Jayne hoped that Labour would win, if only because of a promise to abolish the bedroom tax: this might make it easier to remain where she is, in a house both comfortable and convenient. Eviction is a great fear, second only to losing the children who are her life.

Jayne's love for her children is clear: affectionate and tactile, she says she has learned from the experience of the other two now in care. 'One is nine, the other eight. I see them once a week, every Wednesday. I couldn't look after them. They were playing up, and running away from me. The stress of looking after the household and keeping them under control was beyond me.

'I've been in this house nine years. Before that I was in Birmingham and Darlaston. I don't have a partner now. The two boys have different fathers. I don't know where they are, either of them. They've gone out of my life as far as I am concerned. I don't bother with the Child Support Agency. I was getting maintenance for the two who are now in care – £1.67 a fortnight for one boy, and £10 for the other, who is now fostered. It isn't worth pursuing the fathers of the other two.' [New cases, formerly under the CSA, were taken over by the Child Maintenance Group, which became part of the Department for Work and Pensions in 2013, although the Child Support Agency still deals with cases from before that date. In 2012 the Department claimed that 81 per cent of non-resident parents were paying. The single-parent group Gingerbread pointed out that these numbers included those who paid only a fraction of the sum to which they were liable, and assesses the fully compliant at 60 per cent. Jayne is one of the 20 per cent of parents receiving no support at all.]

'Even if I don't eat, I make sure the children do. I go to Asda, where food is cheapest. I buy vegetables and get four milk tokens for each child as part of my tax credits. I make spaghetti Bolognese, chicken, mash and vegetables. Brett has anaemia, so he ought to have a special diet.

'I enjoy being with the kids. We listen to music, watch TV, play together. Of the two in care, one has settled down with his foster parents, but the other one gets upset when he comes here.' Jayden, talking to Brett, often calls him 'Sam', the name of one of the boys in care. 'He mistakes him for his older brother', says Jayne, 'because they look alike.'

'I've got a few mates. I have one really good friend, but others have stolen things from me. I don't like the neighbours much. I have a sister in Halesowen who looks after the kids if I have to go to an appointment. I've two brothers, but I don't speak to them. One lives in Cumbria, the other in Devon.'

Jayne says 'I was young when my own mother died'. She doesn't elaborate, but in a simple statement she expresses a sense of maternal loss, which has replayed itself in the forfeit of her own children. It is not difficult to see pain and fear in her anxiety about the two who remain with her.

Jayne returns constantly to the theme that haunts her. 'My son was seven when he was adopted. I had to do it. I couldn't feed them properly. It makes me feel guilty. You tell yourself you are doing what is best for them, you have to.

'I still go to the Jobcentre every six months, although with two small children I'm not in a position to work. In the Jobcentre, they've got rid of all the chairs, so you have to stand. I attend every six months for something called Work Focus, an interview to show I'm ready for work as soon as the children are old enough. Brett goes to nursery from one till four, but by the time I walk back from taking him it's 1.20 and then I have to leave at 3.30 to pick him up.

'I can't save for any emergency: with food, gas, electricity, clothing, every day is an emergency. I want the children to look nice. I don't care how I look – even if I have to go out looking like a tramp.

'The Social Services blame me for the upbringing of Sam and Josh. They visit once a fortnight, and I am scared they have their eye on these two. I would like to have the other two back, but how I would manage I do not know. I have no problem with these two young ones. I think you learn. I know I have to be more firm with them. I only went to Social Services for help, but they left me with no choice. It was only supposed to be for four weeks, while they did a parenting assessment. But now it's permanent. What it was, when I had Brett, the other two went wild. I think it was jealousy. They were all right when on their own. I am making every effort with these two. I do everything right. I love my children.'

These are complicated feelings. A sense of loss and failure are in conflict with a feeling of relief and the certainty that the children in care will be physically cared for. But they won't be *loved* in the same way. 'Childhood', one single mother said, 'is so short, but every day can seem like an eternity between getting up in the morning and going to sleep at night.'

Paula

A similar story of asking for children to be taken into care came from *Paula*. In her early forties, Paula has reflected deeply on her own catastrophically unhappy childhood.

It is a chill April afternoon. The windows in the flat are being replaced, and dust and cold air sweep through the room. Paula's partner, Jimmy, makes coffee and they exchange jokes with the men working on the windows.

Paula is on warfarin for life, because her blood clots too easily. She says both she and Jimmy have 'mental health issues', a vague enough statement, but which becomes clearer as we talk. At first, it sounds like a classic story of contemporary poverty: liable for bedroom tax, they have had to rely on food banks. Their benefits were 'sanctioned', the most arbitrary and unaccountable form of welfare cut, since an elementary 'infringement' of rules (many of them opaque to those on benefit) can lead to months without any income. The effects of this are passed on to other agencies: the NHS because of malnutrition, lowered resistance and the effects on mental health; the police and the courts because of crime; businesses because of theft and shoplifting. Trifling savings multiply the costs felt elsewhere.

'I was claiming as a single person when I came here' says Paula. 'When Jimmy moved in, I still claimed separately. I didn't try to hide it. Then they said we had to be classed as a couple, and we were sanctioned. We received no benefit for 11 weeks. It was hard. That was when we went to the food bank - it feeds you but doesn't nourish you. It keeps you alive. We get cereal, Robinsons juice, tinned beans, pies, potatoes. During that time I hit rock bottom. I took an overdose of all Jimmy's medication. I don't know what I took. I fell into a coma. We had already been selling our possessions – such as they were.

'They gave me an assessment for Personal Independence Payment. The woman who came here never even asked what medication I was on. She seemed more interested in my fish tank than in me. I was turned down. We are now appealing that decision.

'Jimmy gets £172 a month Disability Living Allowance and £258 a month Income Support. My DLA has been stopped. He had a Carer's Allowance for me, but you can't claim it if you are not getting DLA or Personal Independence Payment. Last week I had to swallow my pride and ask for a loan.

'I was born in Ireland, but we came to Birmingham when I was very young. I have a sister in Dudley, but most of the family are in Ireland. We were 13 children.

'As I was growing up in Birmingham, I got involved with a gang. I was young, naïve and vulnerable. I took myself to the police station. They said "Give us names". I said "The day I want a bullet in my head, that's the day I'll give you names." That was eight years ago. I asked the police to move me, and they arranged for me to be settled here. It was the best day's work I ever did. Here I try not to keep friends, because when I have made friends in the past, before you realise it, they know everything about you. I am a loner really. I go to Hawthorn Court, flats for vulnerable adults, to do voluntary work.

'At present, we pay £40 bedroom tax; £27 a month towards council tax. Electricity costs £20 for two weeks, gas £20 for two weeks, water £8 a week, TV licence £11.29 a fortnight. I buy the cheapest food. I can get a tray of lamb chops for £5. When you know what your income is you can budget accordingly. I have to take a taxi to go to hospital, £4.50 each way: I have panic attacks and can't get on buses. I have had these since childhood, but they were identified only when I was 29.'

People sometimes spontaneously offer a bleak, abridged biography; bare facts that serve as an explanation, even an extenuation – of their circumstances. Jimmy's mother was Jamaican; when she died his father married again. Jimmy, who is more reticent than Paula, was diagnosed with depression and anxiety in his twenties. His medication has now been reduced. He says 'I felt there was no hope for me. I couldn't see the light anywhere.'

'I had a horrific childhood' says Paula. 'They saw my behaviour as erratic, and I was sent to psychiatrists. Only when I moved here it was recognised that I have paranoia. I was sectioned. I barricaded myself in the flat where I was living. The police came, and I was referred to the hospital.

'But still there is pressure put on us to work. I was on Employment and Support Allowance. I was called to a medical in Birmingham. They asked "Can you do this? Can you do that?" They saw how swollen my legs are: I am liable to deep-vein thrombosis because of my blood condition. They told me I was fit for work.' The Work Capability Assessment is difficult to apply equitably: those judging other people's fitness for work apply limited criteria, and fail to take into account the context of their lives. They form a view on the performance of a few simple, physical tasks, and affirm a capacity to work, knowing nothing about the availability, or even the existence, of the jobs that might obtain.

Paula has attempted suicide three times. She wanted to drown herself in Barley Reservoir. She took an overdose, and then made an attempt to hang herself. 'It's struggle, struggle, you wonder what tomorrow is going to bring. Whatever it is, it can't be anything good.'

Jimmy says 'Even if you feel no hope, you think, "Well, maybe I should hold on a bit longer." I got strength from the Jehovah's Witnesses at Kingdom Hall. They got food for me. They showed love. My brother and all his family are members, including his two beautiful children.

Paula has no time for the Witnesses. 'They came here, Valentine's Day. There were two big cards on the shelf, one from each of us to the other. They don't believe in it, or in Christmas or in any celebration. They said "You don't send cards to show love." We are not married and they didn't like that either. They asked questions like "Are you intimate?" They try to brainwash you. They gave us a book to read. They don't allow you to give blood. I've had transfusions because of my clotting, sticky blood syndrome it's called. You can't expect me to believe something like that when other people's blood has saved my life. Jimmy's brother is a full believer.'

Jimmy says 'Jehovah's Witnesses think it is wrong to accept blood. They say you should have faith in Jesus Christ. That made my faith go down.'

Paula responds 'I believe in God. He gave his life for us and all that. But if one of my children needed a blood transfusion, I'd rely on doctors, not faith.'

Paula has five children. All are with foster parents, because she couldn't cope. 'It's hard, but it's best for them. One has a separate father from the four others. The four are mixed race. Social Services gave me a lot of crap. My 14-year-old daughter – her father is white – sent me a letter. She wrote down all her feelings, but I know she could never do it herself, somebody must have done it for her. She said things about my childhood that I had never told her. She posted a picture on Facebook, together with the son of her foster parents, and she left a vile message, holding up a flag of the English Defence League. She says she hasn't got any Paki brothers or sisters. She is angry because I can't give her money.

'I went to Social Services of my own choice. I was in a violent relationship before I met Jimmy, and suffered mental, physical and sexual abuse. I told Social Services it might be best if I put them into voluntary foster care. I battled with them for years. They knew about the violence and I begged them for help. The four are all together, thankfully. My eldest is now 19 and has her own flat. The others are in Oswestry in Shropshire.

'I don't dwell on the past. If I did, I would go under. I was sexually abused by my father. Both my sister and I were attacked when I was eleven and she was 13. We were raped by him. He beat us first. Young as we were, we went straight to the police station. We were so petrified we wet ourselves. Our faces often showed the marks of the buckle of his strap.

We told them at school that our father was touching us. It went on for years. Eventually our grandparents – his parents – took us away to live with them. So afterwards, we stayed with them. But you are scarred by it for life.

'My grandfather died when I was 21. He never spoke to my father from the day he found out what he had done to us till the day he died. At his funeral, my father sat on the horse-drawn hearse and helped carry the coffin.

'Our father used to threaten us. He said to my sister he would cut her tongue out and stick it where the sun don't shine. When she was 17, he took her into the country, tied her to a tree and raped her again. She became pregnant as a result of that. So my sister's daughter is our own sister. He did nine years in prison for that.

'My mother was scared of him. She did leave him and went back to Ireland, taking my younger sister. But he found her. She was so frightened she came back with him.

'When I had counselling, even the counsellor was in tears. My sister and I share everything and I am still close to her. There is a twist in the story: the birth certificates of me and my sister are different from the others. On mine, it says I was born out of Ireland, while on my sister's, where it says Name of Father, there is a blank. We believe that she and I were not his children. That is why he punished us, and felt he could do what he wanted, because we were not related to him.

'I saw him at my mother's funeral in 2011. I said to him "Why?" He said "Are you still going on about that all this way down the line?" They have no idea what damage they do. After the funeral he said to me "Come here Paula, and give me a kiss." I couldn't believe it. I said "I'll come and kiss the headstone when you're under it."'

In the light of such experience, the intervention of the State in withholding an income necessary for survival appears more than punitive: it is malicious. Paula's father was indeed punished for his abuse, but nothing has been done to assist his victim. Quite the contrary – her allowance has been cut and, for a period, withdrawn, while she has been declared fit for work. This is the opposite of the kind of acts of restitution that such victims need if they are to participate meaningfully in society. Experience like Paula's demonstrates the distance to be travelled if any of the government's fine humanitarian words are to be put into practice: much of the disadvantage of those who possess little or nothing is barely remediable, and flimsy rhetoric about 'equality' only adds insult to injury. When they become victims of further punishment, this shows a deeper bankruptcy than any conceivable financial 'deficit': it demonstrates a corrosion of humanity itself, poisoned by the supremacy of money and the subjection of everything to its unappealable judgement.

Violence against women

More than half the women I met had been abused, mistreated or physically hurt by husbands, partners or fathers. All were from among the poorest, where the patriarchal sensibility, officially abandoned elsewhere, finds a refuge. The women who had suffered were by no means all of an older generation. Paula had, even as a child, gone to the police; but many women were never taken seriously, and cited the reluctance of police, until recently, to become involved in what they dismissed as 'domestic' issues.

It is easier to campaign against violence towards women than to penetrate the hidden worlds of shame, misplaced loyalties and secretive family relationships. In June 2015, the Crown Prosecution Service published figures showing that about 107,000 cases involving violence against women had led to prosecution, of which 78,773 resulted in a conviction, a rise of 16.9 per cent on the previous year. Paula was the only women I met who had seen the man who harmed her prosecuted.

It seems there has been a shift in the nature of male violence: in the industrial era, it was common for men to hit their wives – a backhander, a thump or even a punch – and to beat their children, sometimes with a strap or a stair rod. It was also usual for men to demand their 'conjugal rights', which they often did with oafish and brutal directness. Marital rape became an offence only in 1985. Sexual abuse occurred widely, but *was not necessarily recognised as such*. The laws of coverture (in which a woman's legal entity was subsumed in that of a husband) were eroded during the nineteenth century but never formally abolished, so that the ghost of coverture haunted the struggle for women's freedom for generations. Among the poorest, male supremacy is tenacious; it also finds a home in many migrant communities – even second and third generation – especially among the relatively ill-educated.

Shifts in the nature of male violence may be glimpsed anecdotally in women's testimonies. This does not mean we can make general statements about social change and male brutality, but violence against women is bound to be inflected by shifting social values. In a more highly sexualised era, it would not be surprising if it takes on a more overtly sexual nature. This remains a matter of speculation: since so much was concealed in the past, or not articulated, it is impossible to know for sure. Nell, now in her mid-seventies, talks about her first husband. 'I was married to him for 33 years. He used to knock me about. He said he loved me, but if he did, he had a funny way of showing it. I tried to leave him, but couldn't. He wouldn't let me. I'd go to my mother's, and he would come and plead, and I'd have to go back to him.

'When I first met him, he was so handsome. He was in the army. He used to say to me "If my character was as good as my looks, I'd be perfect." I should have taken that as a warning. At first, it was good. Only when he started to drink, everything went wrong. He preferred drink to work. When he did work – and he was employed in metal presses – they said he was a good worker. But he'd do it for a few days and then go on the drink. Then he became another person. One night he came in from the pub. I'd put the kettle on to make him a hot drink. He picked up the boiling water and threw it over me. I was wearing only my nightie and a thin dressing gown. I ran out and went on foot across town to where my mother lived. Of course, she had already been in bed a long time, so I sat in the outside toilet until she woke up in the morning.

'He came and took me home. He pleaded. He said how sorry he was. I could not leave him. "Come back." I felt I had no choice.

'I was with him until he died. He went to hospital for a biopsy on his throat, because they suspected throat cancer. I went with him. I stood at the bottom of the staircase, while he smoked a cigarette. He said "You go home now, there's no point in you coming back into the ward." I said "I'll see you tomorrow." He said "If I'm still here." "Oh, you'll be here." Before I went, he looked at me and said "God bless. I love you."

They were the last words he said. He died of a massive heart attack while he was under the anaesthetic having the biopsy.'

Nell married a second time. She had known her second husband for some time before they were married. The second marriage lasted only two years. 'But it made up for everything. I do miss him. He said he would give me the sun, the moon and the stars. We were both dependent on wheel chairs and I knew he had a bad heart. We hesitated before deciding to live together. But then we thought "What have we got to lose?" and he moved in. I felt so well loved during that time.'

When he died, Nell's disability benefit was stopped, but the money adviser of the housing association where she lives made sure her entitlements were reinstated. Nell cannot go out: her rare trips are either to the doctor or to the hospital. She sits with her legs on a footstool, because ten years ago she had a knee replacement, but was allergic to the plastic. It had to be removed, and a metal plate inserted, with the result that she has no kneecap, and cannot bend her leg. She has a long scar – about 40 centimetres long – from the outside of the upper leg down to the shin bone.

Nell says 'both husbands were called George, both were born in April. But there was a world between them. Women wouldn't put up with what I did. When I went to the police, they didn't want to know. They said "There's nothing we can do. If he hits you in the street and there were witnesses, it's an assault." Otherwise, it's a "domestic". My mother said to them "Has she got to come to you with her head tucked under her arm before you'll do anything?" They said "I'm afraid so."'

Nell is a generous-spirited woman. She says the two years of happiness erased the memory of the pain she had endured. 'Because I thought I had no option, I suffered less than if I'd known there was something I could do about it. But in working-class life then, you knew so little. I worked all my life, in a factory, and an engineering works. Later, I worked as a cleaner in the hospital. I loved it. I would like to have been a nurse, but had to leave school because the family needed the money. That's the way it was then.'

Men who, two or three generations ago, were used to being, not only heeded, but also obeyed, have lost status. This has turned some into mere wraiths, unsure of their role; others have become serial deserters and fugitives. Some, angry at their loss of social function, sick at heart and in the spirit, resent the forfeit of the power they exercised tyrannically over women and children, and look for other ways of expressing it.

As a result of this, responsibility for family survival has passed increasingly to women, who now make the primary stand against poverty and injustice. Women know they must take control, face the world, challenge bureaucracies, employers and authorities, in order to receive what they and their children are entitled to. When men formed trades unions as an expression of solidarity at an earlier moment in industrial society, women had no such collective unity; only a sub-political solidarity linked their destiny. In a ghostly replay of industrial society, women must now confront men's growing impotence in the labour force and their rage at their loss of status.

Faraji

Abusive relationships are, of course, common to all cultures. *Faraji*'s testimony aroused echoes of our own past, particularly the sense of resignation of women. She came to Britain in 2012 to study, but was also fleeing a violent relationship. Originally from Kenya, she and her husband were living in Tanzania. If it sounds dramatic, to change continents to avoid a brutal relationship, it was. She had been kept virtually a prisoner. Her husband locked her in the house while he went to work. Elegant, enigmatic and serene, she says 'My life stopped when I had children.' She had been studying to become a chartered accountant, but this ceased as a consequence of her marriage.

'We women tolerate being mistreated by men. We are so forgiving. We blame ourselves. There is nothing we can do about it – we are engineered like that. I was not able to leave the relationship, because I believed he could change, just as I believed I had an unlimited capacity for love and forgiveness.

'He was so different from my father. My parents love one another unto death. God blesses certain families, independently of their background. It was my misfortune to meet that man. He exercised complete dominance: he tore up my educational certificates, and piled all my clothes into his car when he went to work, so I could not dress attractively. I had to wear the same things all the time, so I looked shabby. It was a mix of jealousy and control. Part of it is culturally determined – it is expected that men will treat women in that way; but not to that extent. He would explain to people "I have to lock her in the house, because I found her on a cliff, about to throw herself off and kill herself. She will get up and go out in the middle of the night." None of this was true.

'My father urged me, "Go, go." But I was so forgiving. For 15 years. Of course, it all began very beautifully, as love stories do, and you think it will last for ever. Some of these things – call it hope – are in the genes of women, regardless of educational attainment or social origin. The only thing that changes a woman is when her children are in danger or harmed in any way. Then they become fierce and will do anything to save them.

'You think your love will transform the man. For your sake, you believe, he will cease to be himself and become another person. And because of that conviction, we continue to forgive, not once but a hundred times. There is something about you people, men, that makes marriages break up. Men are liars, liars, liars.

'I had a university place in Britain. But my suffering had made me ill, I was too sick to concentrate. I was not functioning properly. I was still taking medication, and although I feel much better now – more free – I don't want to go back to books again. I am at Birmingham University, trying to fulfil my assignments, but it is not helping my state of mind.

'I truly want to work. Being on benefit is not my background, nor what I want to do. I am, of course, grateful for whatever I am given. To me, this is paradise. I appreciate very deeply everything here. When I hear people complain, I want to say to them "Be grateful, say thank you for what you have. There are so many places in the world where you would be on the streets, neglected and ignored if you have no family." I see people on benefit complaining. I hate it.

'I am naturally frugal. It is hard for me to throw food away. I shop very carefully. I go to the shops after four o'clock, just before they close. I also buy fresh food. I cook for myself, and I can make one cooking last three days. If I am given anything, my first response is always to say "Thank you".

'I have a problem with my heart – I am still grieving over the separation from my husband. When we become attached to someone, separation is like a death. It is a bereavement, and the grief goes with you everywhere. I lost so much weight and became very skinny. Once the separation is over, you think you will get it out of your head. But it doesn't go away. It remains. Torture is not an event – its effects follow you. I am an intelligent and able woman, but he told me I was stupid. I do not know if he is more intelligent than I am. He thinks so.

'Of course many things are better here than in Kenya, but I miss the light and the warmth of home. I am safe here. I have learned the ambiguity of things – everywhere there are horrible aspects of life and wonderful experiences. I know it is possible to be intelligent in one way and unaware in others. Professors who know a great deal can be emotionally stupid. We are all both wise and foolish at the same time.

'When I apply for a job, they ask me at the interview what experience I have. I say that I am an accountant, but have no experience. So that avenue closes. I am living alone. I enjoy it. For the first time in many years I am at peace. I don't want a man in my life, certainly not at the moment. I am trying to find myself, the self that was lost in him. I know that when I see my children again, I will be a different person – not an ill person.

'I am fit for work. I would do care work, but I have a back problem and cannot lift people. I don't think I would be very good at it, because when I share people's sorrows, I bring them home with me. To do that kind of work successfully, you have to leave everything behind.

'I want to remove anger and bitterness from my life. To me, education is knowing how to deal with people in the world. It is not diplomas and doctorates. My father is a doctor. I think parents always see their children as the infants they were. I remained a baby to them. And my grandmother – now in her nineties – treats my father the same, as though he were still a child. You never grow up to your parents.'

Faraji – her name means 'consolation' – shows me on her mobile phone a picture of her grandmother's birthday celebrations in her village in the Aberdare Forest – one of the scenic marvels of Kenya, although much damaged by illegal logging and charcoal-burning. The grandmother's house is plain and unadorned. Faraji is sad that she has lost contact with her culture: her knowledge of the language has lapsed, and traditions and customs have faltered in transmission. She gave her 'shoshu' – grandmother – some money for her birthday. She shows me a photo of the old lady spitting on the notes. 'I said "Why is she spitting on the money?" My father laughed and said "That is a blessing." I went to hug her. This was quite foreign to her – in our culture we do not touch each other. I have been brought up in the city, and have come far, culturally, if not emotionally, from those I love. My grandmother does not know her age. They never counted the years, nor celebrated birthdays.'

It is a poignant moment: here in the West Midlands, looking at pictures of a village in another continent, with all the pain of love and estrangement of a woman in exile; a woman who has run away from a violent partner and is now looking for work in a city of which she had scarcely heard until two years ago.

'I smile at people in the street in order not to think about my life. You would be surprised how many people smile back. You get back what you give. I'll heal myself. It has helped, simply being here. If I had stayed at home, I would have been sucked back into the situation with my partner.

'I am not familiar with our traditional culture. People take a carrot out of the rich volcanic soil and eat it without washing it. I would be horrified. But they don't get ill. I miss home. I use all my money up, calling them – an expense that no one allows for. But I fill myself with hope every morning. I say to myself "This is going to be an amazing day." My religion is very important to me. When I first came here, I went to a Church of England. The preacher did not move me. The service was cold and unemotional. I watch and listen to a preacher on YouTube. He speaks so powerfully. He is an evangelical. I like to hear someone talk about the joy of living.'

'Doing the right thing'

The rhetoric of all mainstream parties in recent years has focused on mythic figures – virtuous people 'playing by the rules', 'doing the right thing', 'hard-working families'. This is aimed at majorities, designed to flatter them into believing they are hard done by, victims of injustice. Whenever the secure and self-satisfied are cajoled in this way, it is usually in order to enlist their support for spectacular acts of injustice done to some minority or other; and there are plenty of those in Britain – benefit claimants, refugees, migrants, the mentally ill, people with disability; all of whom have, in some measure, been offered as a foil to groups who see themselves as victims of oppression, 'the taxpayer' being the most sentimental form of humanity conceivable in the mind of Conservatives. Usually male, his devotion to duty is exploited by hordes of welfare claimants, smoking and drinking in the fug of their overheated council houses, while he trudges out every day to struggle with other commuters to reach his site of heroic labour. This image of the taxpayer looms large in political iconography, and welfare recipients are said to batten on him. This distracts from the far more sinister and significant exploitation of the taxation system by transnational corporations, Google, Starbucks and British American Tobacco among them, whose adroit manipulations enable them to avoid taxes altogether.

If hard work, decency, 'aspiration' and commitment were actually guarantors of reward, government would not need to praise these characteristics with such shrill insistence. This refrain mocks those who have followed all the prescriptions, and yet still find themselves brought into poverty or disgrace. Such people show why the welfare state was created: because unforeseen afflictions can strike anybody without warning or notice. Provision must exist for the blameless casualties of society, just as a cushion should also be there for the apparently culpable, for the distinction between the two is far less clear than the clamorous moral certainties of politicians would have us believe.

Grace and Richard

A modern ground-floor flat in the suburbs of the city. Close to a church, the grounds are well kept, and the autumn colours of plane trees and maples give the area a tranquil, almost rural, air. In the flat of *Grace*, in her forties, and *Richard*, 51, everything is in order, and all appears comfortable and in its place. Their experience would have embittered many. Grace says she is 'laid back'. This means she has not complained about the wrongs she has suffered at the hands of the bureaucracies and 'caring' institutions of the State. Grace gets up at three o'clock in the morning every other day, in order to undergo a four-hour dialysis at home: this is so she can take advantage of the cheap electricity tariff, since it becomes far more expensive in the daytime.

Grace and Richard feel cheated; having lived in a four-bedroom house which was too big for them, they thought they were being socially responsible when they downsized and moved into a two-bedroom flat. Grace had kidney failure 20 years ago, and Richard also has a disability.

'I was on dialysis, and had to go to hospital every other day for the procedure, which lasts four hours. The hospital authorities persuaded me to do it at home. They talked me into it, because they realised I am an intelligent person, quite capable of setting up the machine and following the necessary steps without supervision. This, I was told, would free up a bed for the elderly, or those incapable of doing it for themselves. I was an ideal candidate for home dialysis.'

'We were talked into it', Richard says, 'or rather, we were hoodwinked'.

'They told us we would be generously reimbursed for the water and electricity used. There would be no need to worry about the expenses, even though the machine does use a lot of energy. We have tested it, and we know that the allowances are not to our advantage. Far from it. It is a long and tedious business, sitting in a chair, having your blood taken out and passed through the machine. You get very cold, so you have to turn the fire on. I'm shivering all the time, but always aware of how much electricity the heating and the machine are eating up.

'It should have been more convenient. Perhaps if you are working, it is. But I feel out of sight, out of mind. I am helping cut costs for the NHS.' There is, insists Grace, nothing wrong with that, but if those costs are transferred to patients, it is a form of privatisation by stealth.

'It is not for the convenience of the patients. Not only do we make a loss, but it takes time to set up the machine – you have to add half an hour on each side of the actual period it is working. When you go to the hospital, the machine is all ready, you don't have the responsibility of making sure it is in order. Then afterwards, you have to see that the bleeding has stopped before you can go about your day. And then it is all so exhausting.'

Richard was in full-time employment when Grace suffered kidney failure. She was 33. She had a kidney transplant, which lasted seven years. 'That time was a bonus, because the children were still young.' Richard used to do car-valeting. To adapt his work to Grace's needs, he became self-employed, but could not earn a sufficient income and take care of her at the same time. 'I started my own business at the wrong time. I thought I was doing it for the best. You can never tell how things are going to work out.' Again, they were doing the right thing; but the promised outcome failed to appear.

Grace spent a year going to hospital for dialysis. She was given 12 weeks' training to do it at home, and has taken care of it for almost three years. 'Since I've been on dialysis, it has come to light that I have damage to the heart. There is a problem with the valve. I have a slow heart rate and my blood pressure is low.

'Because of my two conditions and David's disability, it seems we are never away from hospital or doctor's appointments. We also feel cheated by the bedroom tax. It isn't a bedroom, it's a medical room. I am doing something to take pressure off the National Health Service. We've done our bit – we got out of a house that was too big, and we took responsibility for my treatment. And we are penalised for it.

'It costs between £250 and £300 a session in hospital – I'm saving the NHS that. I have been very quiet, never created a fuss. But if I call them with a question, they don't phone back. This puts the onus on Richard. He has also been trained, so he knows what to do in any eventuality.

'Last week I called the renal nurse on account of this heart problem. Twelve months ago, because I had a persistent cough, they gave me an X-ray. They found I had an enlarged heart and pulmonary oedema. The department said it would let the renal doctors know. "Leave it with us." For a few months nothing happened, then when I called, the renal nurse said "Oh, it's to be expected when you are on dialysis." No one had ever told us. We had plodded on for 12 months. The cardiologist said "having dialysis doesn't do your heart any favours".'

Grace's original transplant gave her seven and a half years of active life; which continued until 2010. 'To have a transplant you have to be in tip-top condition. I was on the list for another one, but when they discovered my heart was not pumping properly, there was no question of a major operation. I am contacted weekly by the heart nurse: with the renal problem, it's put up and shut up, but the heart has the nurses running around. It seems there is no co-ordination – one department does not know what the other is doing.

'It was better when I went to the renal centre, because I saw doctors and nurses each time. They were monitoring my condition. Now I feel abandoned, at the end of a telephone line that doesn't respond.

'After I had finished the training to do the treatment at home, I complained about something. The sister referred me to a psychiatrist. I went. He said "There is nothing wrong with you."

'The housing association should reclassify this flat; but if they do, they'll lose rent. Housing benefit will step in and question it. We are on benefit, but we budget intelligently, and we can actually afford the money for the bedroom tax – it is the principle, the fact that it is not a spare room. We feel cheated.'

Richard has arthritis of the spine, the hips and knees. He wears a knee-brace. He has tried alternative therapies, including acupuncture. There is little sign that any of these have helped.

Grace receives £127 a week Income Support, and Richard has a £61 Carer's Allowance. She has medium-level disability benefit, £200 a month, and they get housing benefit. They are not required to contribute towards council tax. 'Every time we go to hospital, parking costs a minimum of £3; and if you have to wait for your appointment, it can be much more.'

Grace and Richard have two children. Their son is with his partner in a new relationship. When he comes home, he has to sleep in the living room, because his mother's medical room is not usable for sleeping. The son had a baby with his former partner. He was born brain-damaged, as the result of a faulty delivery in hospital. The child lived until he was three.

Grace feels trapped. 'You can't imagine how tedious it is, sitting in the medical room, knowing that I am paying for the privilege. Electricity is more expensive, because we are on the key. That's why I do dialysis in the dead of night, when it is cheaper. We don't really sleep much. Sometimes I watch a film on my computer, or surf the net, but every other night our sleep is interrupted. We can't go on holiday. You can actually get dialysis if you go away, you have to organise it with the nearest hospital to where you are staying. We did intend to go away last summer, but the effort, simply of administering day-to-day life, is exhausting. You have no energy left. So we did nothing. Even day trips take too much out of me. I feel like a prisoner.'

Richard says 'We try not to live life on a perpetual downer. We like to think of what we can do, rather than what we can't. I get my disability allowance once a month, but much of it is already spoken for. The car needs constant attention. I calculate that with the dialysis we are at least £20 a month out of pocket over the electricity and water needed for Grace. The hospital estimate is that it costs £1 a session, but we know it is much more than that. Our water bill has gone from £70 a quarter to over £100.'

Richard and Grace show me the 'spare' room. The dialysis machine and the big leather chair in which she sits occupy half the space. There is a big cupboard, with dressings, antiseptics and other medication.

'That is not the end of the story' says Grace. Richard is still paying money back to the Social, because when he was classified as disabled, he took a job that was a higher grade than his disability allowed for. He was accused of fraud. It was at the time when everybody was talking about getting people with disability back into work. He took the job in good faith. It will be another two years before that debt is cleared. 'You try to do everything according to what being a good and responsible citizen means, and you are penalised at every turn.'

Later, Grace and Richard's son separated from his partner. He returned home. They no longer have to pay bedroom tax; but their son still has to sleep in the living room.

'It can happen to anyone'

The government insists it has set out 'a new contract with Britain'. Its incantation is: 'Britain is moving from a low-wage, high-tax, high-welfare economy to a higher wage, low-tax and lower welfare economy.' This is magical thinking. The proposal to raise the minimum wage (tendentiously rebranded as 'the living wage') to £9 an hour by 2020 was to have been accompanied by a reduction of in-work benefits, which the Chancellor – under pressure from all political sides – later announced would not take place. One conspicuous element lacking even in the most benign wage legislation is the presence of trade unions and workers' organisations. As well as trade union 'reforms' (that same treacherous word), it seems the government wants to make the unions superfluous by relying upon its own law-making to address social injustice. The freezing of public-sector pay and in-work benefits, and the appropriation of wage-setting by government, de-powers workers and banishes collective bargaining into the realm of theory. In any case, many employers in the low-paid service sector – hospitality, catering and care services in particular – complain bitterly that their businesses will be jeopardised by such an extravagance as the 'living wage', and that such an intervention is the last thing expected from a government which makes a virtue of its dedication to the free play of market forces.

If the political mantra that hard work and law-abiding conduct ensure a life of reward and comfort were true, fewer people in Britain would have learned that, however great their efforts, they are still unable to provide for themselves and those who depend on them. They rely upon 'in-work' benefits, an annual subsidy to employers which reached £30 billion in 2014. 'Tax credits', introduced by Gordon Brown in the Labour government of 1997, served as a supplement to inadequate incomes, and were designed to relieve the poverty of people working but with insufficient income to ensure a decent standard of living. These credits were available to individuals, childless couples and working families with dependent children, and were calculated according to a number of different 'elements' (e.g. a lone parent element or a disabled worker element). They were payable to any household with an income below £6,420, and were reduced by 41p for every £1 above that amount. 'Child tax credits' to the full amount were paid to those with children who were receiving Jobseeker's Allowance or Income Support, and to working households until the income reached £16,105; after which it would be reduced by 41p for every extra £1.

In the July budget of 2015, it was announced that the threshold for tax credits would be dramatically reduced to £3,850 from April 2017. This was subsequently annulled; but the introduction of Universal Credit will retrieve much of the reduction planned for tax credits. All calculations are in flux, since the transition to Universal Credit is proving more laborious and complicated than was expected. However this is resolved, it will be awarded at a lower rate than existing benefits, thereby increasing the contribution of the poorest to 'deficit reduction'. Many people I met expressed extreme anxiety about an expected reduction in their income in the coming years. 'I dread listening to the news' or 'I don't read newspapers' were common responses, since people would rather not know the bad news for them and their loved ones in every fresh edict or policy announcement.

Andrew

Another group of exemplary citizens thrown by misfortune onto the contrived parsimony of the State are those who have 'done the right thing', according to the high moral principles enunciated by government, and have then found themselves unable to work through accident, disability or sickness. They soon discover they get scant recognition, however exemplary their previous conduct.

Only three years ago, *Andrew* was earning £64,000 a year. Now he is in a one-bedroom social housing flat, to which he moved in order to avoid liability to bedroom tax in his former home. He is one of the rare individuals subject to this tax who have managed to find smaller accommodation (about 6 per cent in 2014).

He came to Wolverhampton in 2013, having been made unemployed twice in four years. He has seen the difference in living standards between the comfortable and the poor, having experienced both.

'The first time I was made redundant I was living in Salisbury. At that time, the Department for Work and Pensions were helpful; they assisted you until you found work. I had no previous connection with Wolverhampton. I applied to a company here and was offered a job. I have had extensive experience in my field. I am – I was – a factory manager in Salisbury, and my salary was £64,000. Now, as an unemployed man, I'm getting £72 a week, with £31 disability allowance. My Personal Independence Payment is £74 a week. I am living on £700 a month. That is one-seventh of my former income.'

Andrew is a survivor. He started off poor in life, and going back to it is less of a shock than it might be for people who have never known poverty. 'I was brought up in Glasgow, nine of us in a single-end house. That means a one-room apartment. We slept seven in a bed, four at the top, three at the bottom, head to toe. We learned to look after each other. The building was crumbling. Eventually, we were moved to a big housing scheme in an outer part of Glasgow. We were brought up to a culture of work. We all started as soon as we legally could, and unofficially, even before that. I worked on a farm van from when I was eight; and by 12 or 13 I was working in my non-school hours for a local shop, helping to bring money in.'

Andrew left school at 16 and started in hotel administration, which lasted for six years. After a year, his mother died and his father walked out. Andrew was the second youngest. There were four other brothers. He was smart and took charge of the household, paying the bills, insisting his brothers paid for their keep, so they could afford the rent. He became, in effect, a surrogate parent, which continued until the brothers married and moved out.

'By 1981, the last but one brother left. The eldest remained. He was disabled. In 1982, he had to learn to live on his own, because I was leaving to take up a job in the food industry. He worked in sheltered employment, one of the Royal Workshops for the Blind.

'My brother's story is sad. When one of his baby teeth fell out, it haemorrhaged and became infected. It left him paralysed down the left side. He came through emergency surgery but had 144 stitches from his lip right round to his ear. He never regained the use his left arm. He also had epilepsy which is now under control.

'I moved away to become process controller in a food factory. I rose to assistant manager, and then, in 1988, manager.

I have been in management ever since, and managed factories for major companies – Allied Bakeries, Northern Foods, Greencore.

'I spent two and a half years in Spain, where I had a bar and restaurant. I had got fed up doing the same thing day in day out and getting no recognition for it. I wanted to work for myself. I'm glad I did it, but I came back in 2005, and was soon working as operations manager for a meat company with royal warrants, providing ham and bacon to Buckingham Palace. After 18 months I was approached by a company in Salisbury. I was factory manager there for four years. The company was crushed by one of the big supermarkets, which squeezed it and lowered the price it was willing to pay. The owner would not give in, and lost his business. The supermarket pulled the plug, and he lost 12 million overnight. You have to put cash on the table before you can even become a supplier to the big supermarkets – two or three million at least.

'The company I came to in Wolverhampton was new. I went into it blind, and it was the worst decision I ever made. The owners were liars and con-men. I have always been straight and moral, and I was shocked by their practices. They claimed their meat was *halal*, and it wasn't. Their attitude was, if the paperwork says it's *halal*, it's *halal*.

'After 16 months I was unemployed. The house belonged to the human resources man in the company, so I was suddenly out of a job and homeless. The court gave me a date by which I had to get out. I went to Wolverhampton Council Homeless Department. They advised me not to move until the last possible moment. Then I was found a property with the housing association. I was out of work, so when the bedroom tax was introduced, I had to move into this one-bedroom apartment. I got rid of all my furniture - £5,000 worth of stuff had to go. The removal people took it off my hands for next to nothing.

'I fell into a depression. I was almost suicidal. I had to tell my family I had lost everything. And I had been the successful one. I got some help from one of my brothers.

'I've been here a year. You just have to get on with it. You live within your means, and survive as best you can. I'm still attending hospital, because I am overweight and find it hard to get around. I can't walk more than 15 or 20 yards. I was examined by CAPITA for my Personal Independence Payment. I had to wait eight months. The assessment was nonsense. I had to go from one point to another, and they saw I could just about walk. You have to get eight points to get PIP.

'I am struggling. I have a friend in the USA who helps keep me alive, subsidises my bills. I was still paying the mortgage on my house in Salisbury. The bank threatened to repossess it, but I managed to avoid that. I applied for a Short Sale – the bank assesses the price and buys it, but since this is always much less than you paid for it, you still have to cover the difference. So I'm still in debt for that. The debt is collected by a company. They park the debt for six months. I made an offer of one-third of what I owed, and they accepted it.

'I'm 55. After I had been out of work for a year, I was moved onto something they call the "Work Programme". You are supposed to attend weekly. It is run by a recruitment agency. They said to me "We can't help you, because you are too professional." Being 55 is also scarcely a recommenda-tion. I've applied for as many as 20 jobs a week, but I'm told I am "too experienced", which may also be a way of saying

I'm too old. I get replies and interviews, but I have too much specialised knowledge.

'My background has always been dealing with people. What they do to the unemployed – I couldn't do it. It is calculated to make them feel worthless and incompetent. I would give energy to people, get them to think differently, go out from the Jobcentre with inspiration. I hated going there in the beginning – they do trivial things, like help you with your CV. I don't need that; my CV speaks for itself.'

Andrew has a disability which produces too many white corpuscles, so the immune system attacks healthy parts of his body – it thinks the muscles are an alien part of it. He also has polymyalgia rheumatica and lymphoedema: he has no lymph-nodes in his legs, a genetic condition. He wears compression socks, because the fluid in his legs doesn't move: it bursts through the skin, leading to ulceration. He must bandage his legs every day. He is also on steroids, because without them he would be unable to do anything: a six-year regime of steroids has made him overweight. He is also diabetic, so although he is more than willing to work – he can't stand his enforced idleness – he is physically unable to do anything like as much as his brain-power would wish.

Lazy categories

The distinction between 'deserving' and 'undeserving' is facile and false. These categories are themselves lazy, and owe much to a long and unreflecting tradition, which would separate victims of existential misfortune – the classic widows and orphans, those who survive into extreme old age and people with obvious physical disabilities – from those who prey on the charity of others, dissemble, or feign some form of invisible affliction. The sturdy rogue and vagabond from another era have passed through time, and now present themselves in the guise of the cheat and the swindler, the skiver and the sponger.

One of the benefits of modernity has been that we are now, at least in theory, aware of a wider range of human personalities and conditions than anything that appeared to the legislators of the Elizabethan Poor Law, or those who framed the law of less eligibility, which sent many frail and vulnerable people to live – and die – in the workhouse.

Yet there has been a determined attempt, on the part of governments in our time, to obscure all that is known about the complexity of human motives and the hidden injuries of life. It ought not to be necessary to canvass sympathy on behalf of people who are frightened, or physically and mentally weaker than their neighbours, the six million who suffer some form of depression, the anxious, the demotivated and the grieving, the lonely and abandoned, the agoraphobic and those who hide themselves away, the ashamed and illiterate, the resourceless and the unloved. Of course, there is no predictable interaction of any of these conditions with the social demands made by the people who suffer from them; but that should, surely, make us more, not less, sensitive to the strategies they devise in order to live from day to day.

It may be that reform of the benefits system was overdue. It is certain that errors have been made, wilful and unconscious, both by claimants and administrators. But a 'reform' that is designed solely to simplify a classification system and return it to the easy binary of the meritorious and the cheating is not only deeply reactionary (the social pendulum always swings to and fro), but, in this instance, profoundly inhuman. A more subtle and knowing form of administering benefits is needed, which can take account of something deeper than the mere situational 'elements' of people's claims upon compassion.

Indeed, the work of allocating benefits, like that of minding the elderly and vulnerable, is severely undervalued, for it is left to the sombre magic of markets to determine rewards for 'carers' whose labour requires tenderness and insight. This occupation demands the highest skills in dealing with the most wounded and fragile people in society. If ever there was a case to be made against the universal adulation of the market, it is here: that the weakness and debility of some should be someone else's business opportunity strikes at our deepest feelings of fairness – that is, of a justice that takes into consideration circumstances which no one chooses. Surely, such work should not be at the mercy of minimum wages (whether or not rebranded as 'living') and the profit motive, but rewarded as befits what used to be called, in another world it seems now, a 'vocation' or calling. This work is perceived as a last resort for those who have no other options. Such labour should be exalted and properly prized as noble and worthwhile, and rewarded accordingly; and that means exempting it from exposure to the abrasive power of *market forces*, an expression which evokes the irresistibility of an almost militaristic coercion.

The present venture of the Conservatives to 'free' people from the shackles of welfare is a continuous ceremonial enactment of the triumph of the successful and powerful over the weak. It is a social imperialism, which values success solely in terms of the market, and has no time for failure; even though without failure, those eager to proclaim their dominance would have no foil for their supremacy. In this way, the poor are locked into a relationship with the rich and strong, indispensable to their wealth and power. No wonder the 'relief' of poverty is so elusive: it cannot, must not occur, lest the poor vanish; for this would leave those who are so proud of their achievements high and dry. The poor must remain, so that they, like the vulnerable and weak, might be punished, but not to such a degree that they disappear altogether. The poor are a protected species; but principally so that they might appear as exhibits in the human zoo, to frighten everyone else into compliance and conformity.

The secret world of 'welfare'

Despite the publicity it has received in recent years, the world of 'benefits' is actually closed – a secret shared between those who administer it and people whose lives it touches. The majority of people find its workings unintelligible and its computations of their entitlements arcane. The goals of the private companies that 'deliver' welfare (are they midwives or errand boys?) are far from objective, since the payment they receive depends – although rarely officially conceded – upon their ability to enable government to present statistics that demonstrate a constantly rising labour force and a diminution of those 'claiming benefit'. The deterrents set up for this latter objective are rarely subjected to public scrutiny; and much is made of concealing certain sensitive figures. In 2015, the Department for Work and Pensions failed to publish the statistics relating to suicide and benefit cuts, until a Freedom of Information request by the Disability News Service in December 2014 revealed that the DWP had carried out 60 peer reviews following the death of 'customers' since February 2012. (That the word 'customers' should be employed suggests that those whose survival depends on the benefits system are akin to shoppers, like those at Lidl or Asda, and is calculated to diminish the status and lower the self-esteem of people already cast down by circumstances.) A few cases where callous or indifferent judgements were made have reached the national press. David Clapson, 59, a former soldier who suffered from type-1 diabetes, died in Stevenage in July 2014, three weeks after his benefits had been 'sanctioned'. He died of diabetic ketoacidosis. There was no electricity left on his card, so he was unable to keep the insulin he required in his fridge. No food was found in his stomach, and in his bank account there was £3.44. In warfare, the death of innocents is sometimes referred to as 'collateral damage'. In the war against the poor, such casualties have not yet received any official designation, since no one can be induced to take responsibility for them.

In August 2015, the Department for Work and Pensions published figures which showed that between January 2011 and February 2014, 91,740 people claiming benefits had died. This represents 692 deaths a week, compared with 222 per week between January and November 2011. The Department was swift to point out that no causal effect between benefits and mortality can be drawn from these figures, which is technically correct. But the fact that 2,380 people died within 14 days of being declared 'fit for work' according to the Work Capability Assessment run by ATOS suggests, at the very least, insensitivity and incompetence in the process. After ATOS, partly as a consequence of criticism (40 per cent of decisions resulted in an appeal, of which 40 per cent were successful), and also of 'threats to staff', bought its way out of the contract in 2015, the US firm MAXIMUS – which has a far from untarnished presence in the US, Canada and Saudi Arabia – assumed the same functions, adopting the same criteria for judging people's capacity for employment. Nine months after this 'new broom' began work, the National Audit Office found the number of completed assessments was below target, that the cost had doubled to £579 million annually, and that there remained a backlog of 280,000 cases six months after MAXIMUS took over from ATOS.

Self-employment as a refuge

The Thatcher government concealed the extent of unemployment in the 1980s by transferring many redundant workers to incapacity or disability benefit. This was not entirely a fiction: the stress of widespread unemployment in communities, the very reason for existence of which had depended upon labour, led many people to psychological and mental breakdown; while an accumulation of untreated illnesses resulting from heavy labour made others unfit for work. But the procedure was effective, and the figures of those out of work remained 'manageable' (a mere 3.2 million in 1984), in that they did not give rise to widespread social unrest.

Since 2010, governments have expressed a determination to flush out those they believe have sheltered behind a too easy appeal to 'disability' as a reason for worklessness. At the same time, they have been eager to show benign unemployment figures. This has been achieved by a different kind of subterfuge. First of all, the pressure on people to work, whether or not they are capable of some form of labour, has been one way, encouraged by the outsourcing to private companies of judgements on people's capacity for work, and also by benefit sanctions, often arbitrary, sometimes capricious, which reduce the numbers of those 'out of work and receiving benefit'.

There has also been, as we know, a growth in numbers who are working part-time, underemployed, or on zero-hours contracts. Whatever the advantage of this to individuals, it is of great assistance in the compiling of statistics. But as one of the principal stratagems contributing to a continuous fall in unemployment figures, there has been collusion with people who register as 'self-employed', even if the work they do produces far less than a living income. They also receive tax credits, and Jobcentre staff are less likely to quarrel with their status than they are with the condition of the avowedly unemployed. The self-employed are not 'seeking work'. Many are seeking more work; but that is another matter. Some unemployed people have become aware of this way out of public obloquy, and have joined the respectable if fragile ranks of those who can claim the proud independence of their all too often impecunious self-employment.

Joshua Ademola

A street in the centre of the Wolverhampton, rebuilt in the late twentieth century as a reconstruction of its nineteenth-century predecessor, but with more space and more greenery. *Joshua*'s small flat is thinly furnished: two rooms hold nothing but books, papers and clothes in cardboard boxes. The main articles of furniture in the living room are a leather sofa (where Joshua sleeps, since he has no bed) and an armchair. Joshua is a slight man, articulate and intelligent, his understanding of the world shaped by a mixture of his Yoruba background and the English class system.

Joshua is from Ibadan in Nigeria, and his roots are in Yoruba culture. When his family came to Britain, they were financially and socially stable, quite affluent. Joshua was nine and he finished primary schooling in Britain. His father worked for Italian and German companies, selling cocoa-processing machinery. They moved back and forth between Europe and Nigeria. His parents paid for his education, because they were convinced a private college would be better than a State school. He was on a student visa and got indefinite leave to remain when he left college at the age of 16.

He says 'I failed miserably. I didn't want to go to that school. I was only just settling into this country, and I was out of place. It set me back. Only recently I realised that I am competent and can do things. I want to return to university, but that needs money I don't have. I left school because I was studying sciences, which I didn't really want to do. Another reason for giving up was because my parents were not around. They had been very strict with me, and when the pressure was off, I had too much freedom. I didn't know what to do with it. I was the youngest in the family, and had more space to be myself than my siblings.

'I dropped out, and tried my hand in the media in TV and radio production. I worked with a youth group and we organised shows. I actually got an award in Birmingham for my contribution as a young Black African/Caribbean. It was very promising.

'Then I decided to go to university. As an immigrant, all the time you are walking on eggshells. I was secure here, but I was always anxious to avoid authority. I went to Anglia Ruskin College in Cambridge. When I applied for a student loan, it turned out the family solicitor had produced fake documents.

I was shocked. I appealed and I took it to the MP, who sorted it out. That took time and I couldn't complete the course. I went back to Birmingham. I got my letter confirming I had indefinite leave to remain, and wanted to go back to university. But it was too late.

'My health is not good. I have sickle-cell anaemia. I was quite weak at that time, and I had no income. My lucky break came when my brother started up a social housing association for the homeless, and he offered me a job. I was fresh from university, and brought a new perspective to the work he was doing. I could research and provide valuable input for him. He was already working with homeless people, and within a few months he was getting a lot of referrals of people who needed shelter.

'His idea was that they would rent rooms in shared houses, so it would not be like a hostel. It was a different psychology towards the homeless – they should live in the same way as everybody else. We rented properties from landlords and then sub-let rooms to tenants. Other housing associations didn't like it. They wanted to shut us down because we had no official funding. It was a not-for-profit business.

'It failed. In the beginning, the phone never stopped ringing. I was living on my own in Birmingham, hard work, sleepless nights. We moved lots of people into new places, people who were sleeping out or who had been turned out of home for one reason or another. It wasn't easy. You would put them in a house just renovated, go back a week later, and find it trashed. Repairs were costly, but we learned to do a lot for ourselves. I enjoyed it.

'That lasted six years. Then the decline set in. My brother is still hanging on by the skin of his teeth, but he could no longer afford to pay me. He won't let it go – that has been his life for 20 years. I had to get away. I applied for accommodation in Wolverhampton. I had a sense of failure. I admire my brother – he has the kind of personality that will not give up.

'So last year I came here. For one thing it is cheaper – you can walk virtually everywhere in the city. I am self-employed, doing property maintenance, which is what I was doing with my brother. I don't have a vehicle – the cost of keeping it up was too high. I have to get business cards printed and draw up a business plan. I would rather be self-employed, because with sickle-cell, my health is unpredictable. I stopped being an employee, because I was sanctioned so many times, when illness prevented me from working. I get pain, and when it comes to a crisis, I can't move, my whole body becomes paralysed. I try not to take too many painkillers. I have been lucky, because I have not had a severe attack for two or three months. It affects the ribs, spine, legs and arms. The sickle cells block blood flowing to the limbs and organs, and that causes the pain. It can be brought on by stress, or even sudden changes of temperature. It can last a few minutes or weeks on end.'

Joshua's work on building maintenance, decorating and property repairs earned him work and tax credits worth £210 a month. This has now been reduced to £190. He pays the self-employed insurance stamp. His rent is £400 a month. He is liable for the bedroom tax, even though the room is poky and unfurnished. His contribution is £55 a month, but he is heavily in arrears. 'If I could let one room, maybe I'd have enough money for the rent, but that isn't legal – it would be a breach of my tenancy contract.' Joshua had an overdraft, which he is paying off at £50 a month. This leaves him £140 as his sole income, because his recent earnings have been negligible. Joshua believes in 'the old-fashioned way of marketing', knocking on people's doors. 'Without work, you lose self-belief. Your mental state suffers. You feel depressed and think things are pointless. As a man, it is not a nice feeling. I have not been to the doctor. What can they do?'

Joshua values privacy and his freedom. He wants to furnish and decorate the rooms to his taste, but so far, has been unable even to carpet them. 'For the first six months I slept on the floor. Now I sleep on the sofa. I use £40 a month for gas, £40 for electricity. I use £20 of phone credit a month.

'How do I eat? I'll show you.' There is no gas stove, but a slow rice-cooker and a microwave. He opens the fridge – the metal parallels of the shelves are bare, apart from five onions, three chillies, a bottle of milk, two eggs and a packet of margarine. Joshua's usual meal is rice with chilli and onion. In the cupboard there is tea and sugar. 'Sometimes', he says, 'my sister gives me a fiver for a take-away. That is a kind of luxury. I prefer to cook for myself.

'Don't get me wrong. I'm grateful to the welfare system, but being on benefit is not a choice anyone would make if they could avoid it. Benefits have to be lower than the lowest-paid worker, but at least I'm not in the workhouse. I'd rather stay self-employed. I am tired of working and then having to apply for unemployment benefit. Because of my health, I'm forced to take weeks off. I'm an unreliable worker. No employer will take the risk. Then the benefit you are entitled to changes all the time, and they hassle you.'

Joshua is typical of a growing number of self-employed people who scarcely make a living. In August 2014, there were 4.6 million self-employed in the UK, 15 per cent of the labour force. These account for two-fifths of the new jobs created since 2010. The largest single categories of self-employed are builders, taxi-drivers and carpenters. In 2014, 2,000 people a month were said to be moving off benefits and into self-employment. Thirteen per cent of the self-employed work more than 60 hours a week. Their median income dropped by 14 per cent between 2010 and 2014 to £207 a week. Their average age is 47; and among them are 420,000 pensioners.

'Before I left Birmingham for university', says Joshua, 'I was proud of myself. I was doing media courses and working with youth groups. I was also working in the evenings, bar work, waiting, office jobs. I was self-reliant and self-confident. A lot of that has gone now.'

Joshua has two brothers and two sisters. His older brother still works with the homeless. The younger is a chemist, but because work is not steady, he is employed in a gym as a personal trainer. Joshua's older sister is a human rights and immigration consultant. The other sister has a good position as a clinical researcher at the University of Birmingham. Joshua's family is like many migrant families, in that, academically, the girls are doing better than the boys.

Their parents are in Ibadan. Joshua's relationship with his father is not good. 'He lost his job with the Italian and German companies without any compensation. He thought he was secure. They are now back in our house. When times were good, we had several properties, which have now been sold. I miss home; only I'm not quite sure where home is – England or Nigeria. The last time I went there was for my grandmother's funeral in 1994. When I was in Cambridge at the time of the World Cup, I said "we" meaning the English team. My British friend said "What do you mean, 'we'"? So in some ways, people make you feel you don't belong. But in Nigeria, I would be seen as Oyinbo, which means "peeled skin" in Yoruba, hence Europeanised. When I lived in Birmingham, it was close to an area known for supporting the National Front.'

Joshua is frustrated. 'If I stop self-employment I'll be in trouble. Even if I get a full-time job, I'd get paid only after a month and would be further in arrears. I suffer from anxiety. I am single now. I don't have a partner because of my economic condition. I don't have the money to sustain a relationship. Any sort of social life is expensive. Fortunately, I'm happy with my own company. When business was good, there were plenty of women around. I think they can smell money. I'd be standing at the bus stop, looking at some girl, and we'd exchange phone numbers just like that. It doesn't happen now. Maybe they can see by my shy demeanour and hunched shoulders that I'm not self-confident.'

Joshua feels he never completes anything. 'I'm looking at possibilities. I'd like to go back to university and study anthropology. It isn't possible. People might think "Oh well, if he got off his arse." But I've tried so many times and failed. I hate the position I'm in. I have to cut down my wants, if not my needs. Imagine a society where all your wants were satisfied!

'I feel separated from my sister who lives in Stafford. It costs £10 for a day return. In this society, you have to depend on money. We have lost contact with nature; the economy demands it. The more you depend on money, the less self-reliant you become. If we provided things for ourselves – food, housing, clothing, the economy would collapse. One thing I have learned is how money wipes out people's ability to do things for themselves.'

On the floor is a pile of letters, some unopened. Joshua says the only post he gets is demands for money. There is a council tax bill from when he lived in Birmingham; a Wolverhampton council tax bill; an unpaid fine for driving a car without insurance which Joshua had borrowed from a friend; another fine for rent arrears from Birmingham council for £1,160. There are letters stamped in red DELIVERED BY HAND; a summons to a magistrates' court; and demands from debt-collection companies with names like RECOVERA or ENFORSA. Joshua says despairingly 'I don't open them. Let them come to the flat and take what they want. I only have a sofa and a chair. The TV belongs to my brother and the computer is my nephew's. I can always go back to sleeping on the floor.'

Self-employment takes pressure off Joshua, although work is scarce, particularly since he lives where few people know him. Joshua is an intelligent and attractive person, but he is caught in a complicated tangle of ill health, the mechanistic operation of the benefits system, and his own reluctance to confront the dire position he is in.

Dayanne: the right thing and the wrong result

Dayanne has five children, all boys, aged from 11 to 21. The father of the first three has long disappeared from their lives, but the father of the younger two is a great support. He employs the 17-year-old in his gym. She is delighted that among her three grandchildren there is one girl.

Dayanne did everything the politicians say she ought to have done. She started her own business, and poured her heart and soul into it. And she finds herself with nothing.

Dayanne was herself one of five children – four girls and a boy. Born in Wolverhampton, she remembers her grandmother saying that when she first arrived in Britain, she walked up and down, knocking on doors, asking for work and accommodation. She eventually found work, like many women from the Caribbean, in the National Health Service. Dayanne's mother struggled as a single parent. 'She gave me everything. I left school at 16 and was taken on as a hairdresser in Smethwick. At first it was work experience without pay, but they kept me on. I loved it, and stayed until I had my first child at 19. I returned to work whenever I could, but I didn't want to leave my young children among strangers. I returned as soon as they were all at school. I was a sales assistant in the House of Fraser in Birmingham until they closed down.

'I went to college to learn to do European hair, because until then I had only done Afro-Caribbean. It is very different. It was a three-year course. I also worked with children. That is what I would like to do now, but I don't have the qualification. I brought up five boys – you might think that was sufficient for child care, but apparently not.

'I didn't do very well at school, and that is why I have always been on my kids' case; only now I am feeling the burn, because without a qualification you can't get a job with children.

'I enjoyed my children. All my boys are fantastic. They have respect for me and respect for other people. Even though it was a struggle, I made them my priority. The three oldest have set up their own business, a vehicle-rescue service; as well as that they do taxi work and delivery driving. It is hard, but they are determined to make a go of it. As long as they are doing well, looking good and not wasting their lives, I'm happy. I had to be mother and father to them. My second husband has been brilliant. I've stayed friends with him. He gets on well with the older boys, too. Their own father has never been there for them.

'Do you know what? I leave everything to God; and I have always got by. I don't go to any particular church, but even when I have not had a tanner in my purse, I've always had gas and electricity and put food on the table. I have to pay bedroom tax, because this is a three-bedroom house, and only two of my boys live here. It couldn't have come at a worse time, because I lost my business.

'This is the great disappointment of my life. I opened a shop in the city centre. I was on Jobseeker's Allowance, and went every week to the Jobcentre. They talked to me as though I was a bum – what have you been looking for, how many jobs did you apply for, what was the outcome, what are you doing with your time? It was intrusive and humiliating.

'I did my best to get work, but without grades from school and training only in hairdressing, it was hard. It was a big decision to start my own business. I decided I'd open a shop not a salon. I had noticed there was no Afro-Caribbean hair shop in the city centre. People had to go to Birmingham if they wanted to buy hair-pieces, accessories and so on. I went to a Chamber of Commerce talk on business ventures and met a guy who said that even if you can't spell your own name, you can still own a business. That gave me confidence.

'I started looking at shops. There were a lot empty. I thought anything is better than going back to Jobseeker's Allowance.

'I saw a shop and made enquiries. The rent was high because it was near the city centre. Most black people who own shops are in the back streets. I liked the idea of coming into the very heart of things. I actually paid £800 to a solicitor, although

I didn't need him. I had a bit of savings, and I explained my business plan to the family. They could see the gap I was hoping to fill, thought it was good idea and somehow we came up with the money. They were generous – just gave it to me and told me to get on with it.

'I bought stock, all the products. I got boards and hooks and an attractive sign for the front of the shop. I paid people to put up shelves. I bought colouring, shampoos, oils, wigs. It became an obsession – my 11-year-old felt a bit neglected. But the work was good. I loved it. I ordered whatever people wanted. I treated the work professionally. It was mine! The business was brilliant. People with mixed race children used to come in and ask for advice, and I gave consultations, because they were not quite sure how to do their children's hair. It would have been wonderful.'

A month after Dayanne opened, a business called Hair International opened, right opposite her store. This is an extensive operation, with branches all over Birmingham and the West Midlands. It is run by Asians, even though they sell black hair and beauty products. Dayanne thinks they saw her shop and directly targeted it.

It hit her business. She decided to turn it into a salon. There was a spare room at the back, so she installed a sink and made plans to open. She engaged an Indian woman to do waxing and threading, and planned to hire a barber for men's hair. She bought floor-covering and a bed for waxing. She had come out of the benefits system, but found demands for money overwhelming. She was ambitious, wanting to serve wine, coffee, chocolate. She intended to do feet and nails as well, and engaged two girls.

She informed the council of the plan. The next day a representative came. He asked 'You haven't made any phone calls yet or started trading?' 'No, why?' 'If you use the back room as part of your business, it'll cost £1,000 on top of the rates.'

'It was the last straw. What with Hair International and the rates hike, with rent, rates and salary, I could not carry on. I closed the shop. It had been just one year – May 2012 till May 2013. I thought to myself "I've still got customers. I'll keep going." I thought I could maintain it as a mobile business, going to people's homes. But some were far away – Dudley, Tipton, Bloxwich. The cost of travelling, the time spent on travel, repairs to the car – I couldn't handle it. I'd had business cards printed, but it was too much. It was also hard to get new customers – people go to a hair salon as a social event.

'I couldn't pay the money I owed. I didn't want to take any more loans. I still kept a few customers, I'm now part-time self-employed, which is the worst of all worlds. I can't go back on the dole. I went for a job interview as a support-worker, but they want training and qualifications. They were offering only £6.50 an hour, but I'd take it, I wouldn't mind. I could do children's residential care. I would be so good at it, but without experience they won't take you. I need a job where I'll get training as I work. I can't afford to go on any course beforehand.

'We all learn from one book; the trouble is, it's the same book. I get child tax credit which comes to £262 a month. I earn about £400 a month. My 17-year-old is working. But you can't do half the things you want to. Then to cap it all, I got a ticket on my son's car, which I'd left outside for all of ten minutes.' Dayanne is a happy personality, but she cries with vexation and disappointment when she recalls the excitement and hope with which she embarked on her business. She wipes her eyes. 'I think my religion is the way I live my life. I think love is the most important thing. My boys know they can talk to me about anything. They all have a key to the house, they come and go as they like. Those awards up there are what they won for Kung-Fu.

'I have debts to pay off. That is what keeps me from doing what I'd like to do. I know I would be so good at looking after children. I'm so proud of my boys. I'm supposed to pay bedroom tax, but they've put it on ice for the time being. Perhaps they understand how I've struggled and done my best.' It was not long before Dayanne got a job; not her first choice because it is in retail. It is difficult to assess the cost to individuals who use up so much energy and commitment in doing precisely what Authority urges, only to find their efforts come to nothing in a society which has no instruments for measuring the effort and pain of people who strive, even in vain.

The roots of alienation

Perhaps the most frequent words I heard in the West Midlands were 'humiliation' and 'respect'. The word 'respect' was used mainly by those who felt its absence in the assault upon their dignity. People feel 'worthless'. Their feelings are disregarded; they are infantilised and treated with contempt by public servants. There is no space to explain themselves and their circumstances. There is no understanding or compassion (a quality David Cameron recommended in 2013 should be 'learned' by health-care professionals). Many experience their treatment as bullying. This, while supposedly an issue of concern, is actually elevated into high principle in the benefits system; and official disapproval of it is perceived by claimants as hypocrisy.

Khaled Siddiqui is 60. He came to the West Midlands from Sylhet in Bangladesh in 1973. His father had been a seaman on a British ship. The family in Bangladesh heard nothing of him for years and assumed he was dead. He had actually been in Britain for 14 years. One day, quite suddenly, he appeared at home. Khaled was in school. The family lived in a village far from Sylhet City, and the whole community turned out to see him, because at that time, few were 'London-returned', and something of the magic of migration clung to them. Khaled was born a few months after his father's departure, and had never seen him. He had come back to take the family to England.

'We had a small piece of land in the village. This was entrusted to a relative, who cultivated it and used the produce to feed his family. I last went back in 2005. In Wolverhampton, my father was working in a copper refinery. We had no idea what to expect. It was exciting.'

For Khaled, his brother and two sisters the excitement turned to shock. He felt the cold, and at that time there were problems with skinheads. They heard of people being attacked in the streets, which created a feeling of insecurity. Unable to finish his schooling, he went to work in a restaurant. As a youngster, he had to start at the bottom, chopping vegetables and watching how things were done. After five years, he rose to be chef. That, he says, was how it was then – you learned on the job, by observing people who had the skills. It was a personal relationship, not theory, but practical. He stayed 15 years until the owner died.

'I went to a restaurant in Tamworth, and was there until 1999. In 2000, in my early forties, my mother died. I was on the aircraft, taking her body back to Bangladesh for burial, and I had my first heart attack. On landing, I was taken to a private clinic in Sylhet City and stayed 25 days. Some relatives came and took my mother's remains, which they buried according to custom. I felt sad I had made the long journey to bring her to her native soil, and then could not perform the duties of a son.

'After another month, I came back to England. I had a second attack two days after reaching home. The third came when I went to Saudi Arabia for the *hajj*. That was in Medina. I had to get a visa extension, because I was too ill to move.

'In 2005, I went with my children to Bangladesh and spent five months there. Once again, soon after my return, I felt a pain in my chest. I was at my daughter's house for Sunday lunch. I fell unconscious in the ambulance and woke up only four days later. I was told it was impossible to have a by-pass, because the first attack had done too much damage – being on the aircraft, it had taken many hours before they got me to hospital.

'I can't do any work, or undertake any activity without becoming breathless. In 2011, my sickness benefit stopped, and they were pushing me to look for work. When I went to sign on, the people at the Jobcentre said "Why didn't you find a job?" It is a great worry to me, because there is little I can do. It raises my level of anxiety, and I am afraid it is going to bring on another attack.

'I live with my son, and I was getting £192 for two weeks. That was then reduced to £143. They stopped accepting sick notes from my doctor. "No", they said "you are all right." They started giving me tokens for the supermarket instead of money.

Mr Siddiqui has an appointment for a Personal Independence Payment assessment with CAPITA. He was initially given an appointment in Nottingham, rescheduled in Wolverhampton, because he could not make the journey. In the meantime, his money has been cut to £123 a fortnight. He is to be seen by a 'health professional'. He has prescriptions, cardiograms, hospital reports, and, fumbling in his bag, produces a sheaf of documents (documents, the bane of poor people the world over; mystifying, written in the hermetic dialect used only by bureaucracies, threatening, demanding, confusing). CAPITA takes no account of his medical history. The 'health professional' is employed by the company, which has an interest in pushing people as 'fit for work', because their income depends on it. Khaled asks sardonically, 'What about the health professionals I've seen over 15 years? You don't invent heart attacks.'

Khaled's son has just started work in a restaurant, after a period of unemployment. The flat they occupy has two bedrooms and the son – who is 25 – is being charged bedroom tax. 'He is my carer. I have to have someone live with me, because I cannot do things for myself. Why should we be expected to sleep in one room?'

Khaled has eight children. All five girls are married, their husbands working. One son is married and working. Of the youngest two, one is living with his father, the second with his mother. They separated in 2007. 'I have to take 14 tablets every morning. We have a debt of £589 owing on rent arrears. And now this bedroom tax has reduced housing benefit from £97 a week to £77. That and the maintenance charge take £18.80 out of our weekly income. We pay £58 a month gas, £40 electricity and £40 water. We can't buy the food we need. We buy rice and make a curry. We don't buy milk or fruit.'

Khaled Siddiqui looks on his 40 years in the West Midlands, shakes his head and says 'This country changes people. Children don't help their parents as they did. They have their own expenses and their own life. My son once said to me when he was a youngster "You owe me ten pounds." That was unheard-of in our tradition, a child telling his father he owed him money. When you have nourished them and brought them up and taught them how to be moral and good citizens, how can you owe them anything? They owe everything they are to the love of their parents.'

Khaled has a damaged heart; but this is nothing to the damaged heart of a benefits system, to which such a story is merely a plea to be excused further labour. It may be pointless to ask how many Saturday night curries he has produced over 30 years, often for people drunk and offensive after a night out, and what humiliations he has undergone in this form of servitude. But it is certainly not beside the point to ask what effect this has had on a new generation, who are not prepared meekly to submit to the privilege of being forced to yield to the imperious demands of those who, in their fuddled arrogance, see themselves as their betters. The roots of alienation – even of radicalisation – may be sought on websites and in the words of firebrand preachers; but we underestimate the effects of experience, much of it degrading and humiliating, in the heart of our own society at our peril.

Imran Noorzai

When I called on Mr and Mrs Noorzai, *Imran* was lying in bed, although it was mid-afternoon. The previous evening, someone had broken into his car, and he had reported it to the police. He had been disturbed, unable to sleep, wondering whether it had been someone with a grudge or an opportunistic crime. Only his Sat Nav was taken.

Imran was brought to Wolverhampton from Faisalabad in Pakistan by his parents who were already here. This was 1966, when he was six. Although half a century has passed, he still feels a rancorous sadness about a father who, he says, treated him unjustly. His parents only wanted him as a source of unpaid labour to do the housework. He remembers, as a little boy, climbing onto a box so he could reach the kitchen sink to do the washing up.

He started work at 15, two days after leaving school. He was apprenticed to a toolmaker. There were 30 people in the tool-room and another 30 in the power-press. He was the only Asian at the time. For ten years, he gave all he earned to his father. He never opened the pay packet, and had nothing to spend for himself.

'My father's father died when he was only four, and his mother died six months later. My parents had nothing when they came here. My father worked for British Steel in Bilston. He had come like all the others, saying "We'll work two or three years, save money, go back, open a shop or start a business." Then they stay on another year to pay for a sister's marriage, then another year for a brother's education or some medical treatment. And then, before they realise it, it is too late. The children are British, you have grown older, you have adapted to a different life; and then, life at home has also not stood still. People there have changed too.

'In the early years, men came alone. It was wrong to force families to split up because the men worked; and the government allowed them to bring their dependants here.

'When I was 21, my father arranged a marriage for me in Faisalabad. I can't say it broke down. It never started. I didn't like the girl. I stayed with my uncle in Pakistan for a year and a half. I couldn't go back without getting married. Everybody would ask what happened. It would look like failure. So he took me to see another girl. As soon as I saw her standing in the doorway, I said Yes. She was pretty and we liked one another.

'I went to Islamabad to apply for a visa for her. Some members of her family had spread rumours that I was not working, it was not a real marriage. At the High Commission, they asked me how long I had been in the UK. I told them I had been to school, college and done training courses for my work there. They granted the visa straight away, but relatives bribed the postman not to deliver the letter, which they destroyed – other relatives, not her parents, who were in favour of the marriage. There is often jealousy in families, a desire for the money they think anyone must have if they have been abroad. I lent her parents £2,000 to buy a shop. They did pay it back, but I lent her cousin £1,700 and never saw it again.'

The wider family intrigued and conspired against him. They constantly asked for money and were envious of the oppor-tunities they believed he had in Britain. They knew nothing of the racism and discrimination, the cold, or Enoch Powell and his 'rivers of blood' speech. Imran lived with his parents in their council flat. His relatives in Pakistan imagined them living in luxury. How could he explain to village people what a council estate is?

'You lead a split life, first generation. It is painful. You live here, but your heart is partly there, then it becomes impossible to leave, because your children have their roots here. Then when you do go back, people know you have a bit of money.

They expect help. If you refuse, they try to steal it. I have seen families fight over it.

'When I came back to Wolverhampton after marriage, the tool-room had closed, so I was looking for work. A friend suggested why not work as a taxi-driver. He was a TV mechanic, working part-time as a driver. He set up a taxi business. I worked day-time for £10 a day, which was good money then. The Department of Health and Social Security caught me working. I told them I was only doing it for a trial, to see if I could do it.

'I went full-time. I worked at night. It was more money, but you see things you didn't know existed – young girls taking cocaine, sniffing glue, working on the streets, men fighting over them. And I was paying the company £50 a week for the privilege. Eventually, I bought my own car and became self-employed. One day, a man asked me to take him to Brighton. No problem. Two hundred pounds. Would I take a cheque? No, I'm sorry. He paid me in cash. But when he got there, he found he had forgotten some important papers. Would I drive him back and bring him down again? No problem. That was £800 altogether. He gave me a thousand – a £200 tip. That is the most money I have ever earned in a day.

'One day, driving home from Heathrow I felt a sharp pain and I was sweating. I was on the M1, I thought I'd stop off at a friend's house in Luton. I knocked at the door. A neighbour came and told me they'd gone to Pakistan. I sat in the car for a couple of hours, then thought I might as well drive home, which I did. I took some paracetamol and went to bed. Next day, I couldn't get up or walk. But it passed.

'Some time after, the brother of a friend passed away. I went to the funeral and collapsed. People thought it was the fright of seeing the body. I was taken to hospital. They said to me "When did you have your first heart attack?" I didn't know I'd had one – that must have been the night I was driving on the M1. I was 35. When I got home, it happened twice more. If you have two heart attacks in a week, they take your licence away.

'I'm 54 now. After that I couldn't work. I was on Income Support. I've had seven attacks till now.

'My wife also fell ill. I took her to Pakistan to see her family. After two weeks, we had to come back. She was bleeding badly from the stomach. She was a heavy lady. I brought her home and took her to the hospital. They could not diagnose what was wrong. One night, I said good-night to her – she had to sleep in a power-chair. She woke up at three o'clock and said she would like something to eat. She said she fancied some fresh fruit. So I cut up an apple and a pear. She ate a little and then said "Call an ambulance, my time has come."

'A combination of her weight, her heart and internal problems killed her. She was 33.

'She had promised to take my body back to Pakistan when I died, since it seemed she would outlive me. But it fell to me to take her back to be buried. I asked my son if he wanted to come with me and get married. He said "No, I'm taking my exams." I asked all four of my children if they had any objection if I got married again. They said no, because we needed someone at home to cook and look after us. I said to my uncle in Pakistan "I want to get married, but I want to see the woman first." He said "You don't see them before marriage."

'I stayed in Pakistan only 20 days. During that time, I buried my wife's body and found a new wife. Four days after meeting, we were married. I went to the High Commission for her visa. They said it would come within two months. When the letter came, my uncle's children tore it up and threw it away. I applied here, through the court. The judge ordered the visa to be issued immediately, since I was working and I had been here for so many years.

'My older son from my first marriage is now a flight manager with an airline. The second is a bit of a trouble-maker. The two girls are married. From the second marriage I have two children, a boy of 12 and a girl, seven. I am registered disabled. I've had a triple by-pass. So far, my benefit has not been touched – you can see all the appliances I have to help my mobility.

'I don't know why I've had the misfortunes I've known. I used to walk from Wolverhampton to Tipton to work every day, carrying a tool-bag and copper pipes. When you have lost your health you think about your life. My mother and father left my brother in Pakistan, while they brought me here to do the housework. My brother was favoured over me. I have known more sadness than happiness. My father still goes to and from Pakistan. He has property there as well as two properties here.

'I have to go to the barbers for a shave, because I cannot do it myself. I can't go to the mosque. I dreamed of having my own business. It didn't happen. I wanted a shop. You cannot choose what you want to do. A higher power determines it for you.'

Farida: the duty of young women

It was a day of dramatic weather: westerly gales and fast-moving showers of sleet; the sun threw shadows and dazzling flashes of light on the city's red terraces; an almost surreal image of these prosaic settlements. The house of Farida's parents is plain, once occupied by respectable white working class. Here, there is a curious sense that the values of neighbourhood and kinship, which many former inhabitants left behind when they moved out of the area, have been inherited by newcomers. These are sustained by networks of family and community, an intangible but real inheritance of the area, the unwitting bequest of those who have gone away to follow their destiny as individuals.

The house is simply furnished. On the window sill, seeds in flower pots are breaking through the soil in pale furls – a last memory, perhaps, of a society in which people loved the earth and cherished the produce on which they depended for sustenance.

Farida offers sweet Bengali tea; as her father talks, he recreates his Bangladesh in this little front room in Wolverhampton. He evokes the Liberation War, the mass slaughter of Bengalis, which brought about the birth of the country in 1971. Mr Islam was then 13. His village was bombed and shelled by the Pakistani army. The people dug holes in the earth as shelters from the shrapnel and exploding ordnance. It was a time of extreme violence, vast upheavals and migrations into India; the unsettling of a country which had agreed to be part of Pakistan at Partition in 1947, but which was turned once more into a colony, since it provided raw materials, food and labour for the more developed West Pakistan.

Mr Islam was already in his thirties when he came here. He was 'called' by his brother to join him in a better life, working in Indian restaurants in the West Midlands. 'My father had died, and my younger brother remained to look after the land.' Mr Islam's work presented him with no urgency to learn English, and his language is still basic. His wife, Aliyah, had even less need to learn, since they live close to family and friends from Sylhet. All their working and social life has been among Bengalis. This is not a wilful reluctance to 'integrate': the 'Indian' restaurant is a site of slightly uncomfortable servitude; the people they deal with – particularly late at night – are sometimes threatening, often patronising. This has made them wary of a 'host' community who are guests in their eating-places; and it gives them a particular view of the people of Britain.

Mr Islam is a slim man, now in his late fifties, with a silver beard. He wears a karakul hat of false lamb-fur. He is quiet; a gentle person who accepts that his life has been dedicated, not to his own advancement, but to providing better opportunities for the next generation. He is self-effacing, and it is easy to mistake his limited English for a lack of intelligence; but his eyes shine with a deep understanding of the world, and the piety and sense of justice which are his principal gifts to his children.

Mr Islam relies on Farida, his second daughter, as interpreter between himself and the world beyond the immediate family. 'I came as a young man, I worked in a restaurant, but now we are in crisis. If you are older, they do not want to employ you. The younger generation have taken over the restaurant business, and they do not want to know you.'

There is a sense of siege among many people who came to the West Midlands from South Asia in the 1970s and '80s. It was not their fault that they did not acquire fluent English; there was little interaction with native speakers, and what there was, in the setting of the restaurant, was highly ritualised. They are now blamed by government for circumstances over which they had no control. It simply didn't matter then if you were cooking or working in a kitchen. Now Authority has turned on them, demanding they give an account of themselves and insisting they go to language classes. Mr Islam does indeed go to classes, but finds it difficult to remember words.

Farida is 17. An alert, intelligent young woman, she is doing A levels in Philosophy, Sociology and Law, and is strongly protective of her parents and their vulnerability. Mr Islam regrets he no longer has the strength of a young man; to be approaching 60 in Bangladesh is to be considered old, but above all, it is to be respected. The lack of regard for elders in British society is a source of puzzlement and grief to people from South Asia.

At the Jobcentre, where he must sign on every Friday – a compulsory profane ritual on the holy day of the week – they are 'disrespectful' to his seniority. It is a deep cultural shock, the dismissive, often hectoring way in which older people are treated. Why would anyone seek to 'adapt' to a society inimical to their idea of a proper regard for seniority?

For the family, the practical consequences of these humiliations are dire. On Jobseeker's Allowance, he has been sanctioned a number of times for failing to seek work with sufficient zeal. 'They don't understand older people. We came here long ago. We stuck to one job and did not learn to do anything else.' Mr Islam was sanctioned from 27 December 2014 until April 2015. 'They said I was not actively looking for work. I can't drive and my English is not good. What can I do? They are asking for qualifications I cannot possibly get.'

The number of people sanctioned, according to research by the *Guardian* in the year to April 2014 was 16.7 per cent of claimants. The official government figure gives a rate of 6 per cent, but this is a monthly rate. The government claims sanctions are 'a last resort', but there is clearly no need of such extremes for Mr Ali and those like him who, inoffensive and law-abiding, find themselves stigmatised for reasons they cannot fathom and are in no position to remedy.

Aliyah has also not learned English. Like most of her generation, she understood her purpose to be at home looking after the children. There are five: the oldest, Noori, is married and lives in Essex. The second, 19, works in a day-care centre, and earns about £100 a week. Then comes Farida, Fahim, 15, and Asma, ten.

The family failed to inform the housing association that the 19-year-old was working. With benefits sanctioned, the family has accumulated rent arrears of over £400. Rent is £97 a week. Farida's child benefit was stopped six months earlier without explanation. This has now been restored, thanks to the intervention of a social worker. It is clear that 'welfare cuts' are arbitrary, following no apparent pattern; and if people do not complain, they will not be restored – even benefits to which they are statutorily entitled. The family receives child tax credit of just over £100 a week, and this, with child benefit for the youngest two, has been their sole source of income.

Stoical and uncomplaining, they have adapted to the decrease in income. Farida says her parents regard themselves as 'a transitional generation'. 'They wanted us to get an education, so we would avoid the difficulties and insults they have endured.' The children become intermediaries between Britain and their parents: Farida translates and Fahim helps fill in forms and provides details required by the Jobcentre. Mr Islam left school at 13. Everything was disrupted for him by the *Muktijudda*, the Liberation War, when as many as three million Bengalis are said to have been killed. The war was followed by famine. The markets were well-stocked with produce, but people had no money to buy the food. The dead were collected each morning from around the market. The people had gone there because that was where the food was. Mr Islam's father worked for the British in Singapore, and returned to what was to become East Pakistan after Partition and, 25 years later, Bangladesh.

'We had some land, where we grew rice and wheat, but during the war, we had nothing to eat, because we could not cultivate it. The land is still in the family, worked by one of my brothers, while the rest of us came to England. When I arrived here, I was shocked by the cold and darkness after the sunlight and warmth of Bengal. But I knew this was the best place to raise my children. There is a *system* here. It may not always treat you well, but it exists; and you can appeal if it is not working as it should. In Bangladesh, there is no system. There is political patronage and there is corruption.

'I always supported the Awami League, the party of Sheikh Mujib ur Rahman, who is recognised as the father of the nation, because it was under his leadership that we attained our freedom. After the bombing, I remember coming out of our shelter and seeing dead bodies everywhere.

'In Dhaka over the past 18 months, there have been political strikes led by the Opposition, including the Jama'at e Islami, the party that sided with the Pakistanis against Bangladesh. The political struggle in Bengal is about the relationship between our Muslim identity and Bengali culture and tradition. There should be no conflict: we are first Muslims, because this is our soul. After that comes the language and culture, because we are Bengali speakers and inheritors of a long Bengali tradition.'

Farida observes 'We are living at a difficult moment in Britain. Everyone is stereotyping Muslims. This area is basically Muslim, and it is peaceful and respectful. Only some boys of the young generation are turning their back on our religion and culture; they are drinking and smoking and taking drugs. But they are a minority. We observe the laws of the country. We do what we know is right in all cultures – respect other people and live honest lives.'

Mr Islam is a proud man who suffers in silence the indignities inflicted by the welfare system. He says 'My future dreams have gone. I don't expect anything for myself, but I want my children to do well, to grow up to be good people and to trust in God.'

His principal hope now lies in his accomplished daughters, but even more so, in his son Fahim. Farida says 'Fahim has his father's brain. He is like him. He wants Fahim to realise all the dreams he had.' The boy wants to be an engineer. It falls to him to redeem the family's ambition. Farida sees it as her duty to take responsibility for the comfort and well-being of her parents. 'I will do anything for their happiness' she says. 'I didn't really work at school until just before my GCSEs. Then one day I woke up and thought I'd better do something about it. So I worked hard, got two As, three Bs and three Cs. I don't really enjoy the subjects I do. My favourite subject is religion. I don't want to be a teacher, which would be the expected pathway for me.'

The family is observant. Mr Islam goes to mosque to pray five times daily. The women say prayers at home. Farida has been given her freedom, and whatever she does will be from her own choice; but that choice will always depend on honouring the values of her parents.

They are fortunate, in that two of Mr Islam's brothers live nearby, and one of his sisters is also within walking distance. All have their own families, so there is a strong network of kin in the streets around. This creates a poignant echo of the former neighbourhood communities of the white working class. Whenever there is need, trouble or affliction, caring hands are available to tend for those affected. It is a sad irony that the spirit of community seems to adhere to the fabric of the streets into which a different population has arrived in the last 40 years; a population which inhabits not only the terraced houses, once the homes of labourers, operatives and workers, but also the values of solidarity and neighbourhood which those who left the area bequeathed to the newcomers. These values, lamented now by those who have abandoned them, do not see them as virtues in the latecomers: 'they all stick together', 'they keep themselves to themselves', 'they all help one another' are the responses of people who have set aside these same practices; although their condemnation is, partly at least, also a measure of the pain they feel at their loss.

These are haunted communities. This Black Country was always a place apart, unlike any other industrial area of Britain; inhabited by small entrepreneurs, whose lives were not so very different from those of their employees. There was a semi-rural sensibility, a place for allotments and smallholdings and animal husbandry; for people who were accomplished poachers, kept pigeons and foraged in the countryside for mushrooms, nuts, blackberries, elderberries and medicinal herbs. Despite the opening up of these closed worlds, there remains a certain separateness in the psyche of the West Midlands; another heritable feature of the locality, observable also in more recent arrivals, the children and even grandchildren of migrants. Most young men, far from being attracted by the epic seductions of international politics, express their attachment to the pull of family, neighbourhood and friendship, which is – for the most part – stronger than the tug of solidarity with co-religionists in other parts of the world.

One group of 18-year-olds I met were all working locally – in a restaurant or a shop, as a security guard or delivery driver, or studying business management at college. Syed, the exception, is to become a professional boxer. He had just won his first fight in London. Their chief enemy is the police, who pick them up routinely and search them for drugs. 'I've been targeted since I was 13. You would think by now they'd know I don't do drugs.' 'They *do* know. That's why they pick on us. They don't touch the dealers. *I* know who the dealers are, so if they don't they are not doing their job.' 'They have a target of young people they have to search, so they frisk us, go back to the station, make a report, have a cup of tea, have a wank and go home.'

Abdur is tagged. 'They came to my house and said "You're under arrest for robbery." I kicked out at them. I have to be in by 9.30 at night, but there's not much else to do anyway.' 'Gangs do run streets in this area. Some deal in drugs, but they are bringing money into the neighbourhood. That's economics, isn't it? But the gangs don't bother us. They look after their own.' Young people here do not call themselves 'British Muslims': 'We are Muslim-British, Muslims who happened to be born in Britain.'

Although a majority of young Muslims in the West Midlands live in sometimes uneasy acceptance of the conditions of their lives, it would be foolish to ignore the elements in their daily social experience that alienate them from British society. While the authorities are busy scanning online sites, networks and cells which lead to 'radicalisation', they have perhaps overlooked many of the influences which predispose – or even propel – some young Muslims to estrangement from a society the discriminatory practices of which damage their families and neighbours: the story of mature women who have raised their children being forced into demeaning positions by Jobcentres; the requirements on venerable and pious members of the community to justify their worklessness, despite an absence of jobs and in the presence of heart attacks, diabetes, infirmity, bullying by police, hostility and rejection – none of this is calculated to conciliate a new generation to the circumstances they are supposed to bless as the highest freedoms. In other words, radicalisation often begins at home; and if there is an absence of secular alternatives to impoverishment, prejudice and contempt, it is inevitable that people will have recourse to other-worldly ideologies of deliverance. This is so obvious it should scarcely need to be said. But such is the obtuseness of Authority that the clear remedies for social estrangement and exclusion are invisible to them; or perhaps ideologically so unacceptable that they would rather drive the whole country into a state of paranoia, forcing the discontented into conflict with something we call 'British values', even when these have ceased to mean tolerance, fair play and sympathy for the underdog, and are identified increasingly with injustice, malice and contempt for failure. The benefits system is a not insignificant contributor to wholly avoidable feelings of alienation and resentment; feelings by no means confined to putative 'extremists'.

Welfare and mental health

The Welfare Reform Bill became law in April 2012, and many of the changes it embodied came into effect one year later. The Royal College of Psychiatrists has monitored the consequences of some of these 'reforms', and found that among a range of people with physical and mental disabilities back-to-work programmes were causing great anxiety. This actually inhibited their entrance into the employment system. In May 2013, a Judicial Review found that people with psychiatric problems were at a 'substantial disadvantage' in the Work Capability Assessment.

As outlined earlier, from the outset there were two categories of people eligible for the Employment and Support Allowance: the Work-Related Activity Group and the Support Group. In the first year of this programme (2009), 10 per cent of people were placed in the Support Group and 26 per cent in the WRAG; 63 per cent were found 'fit to work'. By 2013, 47 per cent were in the Support Group, 19 per cent in the WRAG, and 34 per cent 'fit to work'. This suggests wide margins of error in assessing people's capacity.

As the programme proceeded, the number of people whose benefits were sanctioned rose. Among those receiving ESA, sanctions rose from 400 in January 2012 to 4,700 in December 2013. Of those in the WRAG, 50 per cent have mental health problems; but this group accounted for 60 per cent of those sanctioned (www.rcpsych.ac.uk).

It is clear, according to the Royal College of Physicians, that there has been a lack of understanding and inaccuracy in the assessment procedures. The College also expressed concern about the 1.4 million people in Britain who have learning difficulties. Many such people do not exhibit 'symptoms', and readily become victims of censure and mistaken moral judgements.

It is no secret that a disproportionate number of the mentally ill are homeless. In view of this, it is astonishing how many people with complex needs are thrown upon their own resources. Individuals huddled in greasy sleeping-bags in shop doorways, or squares of cardboard packing cases labelled Bosch or Zanussi, are objects of concern to the police, who, on the urging of 'residents', move them on, when they should be referred to agencies concerned with welfare or rehabilitation.

Luke is a young-looking 45. He has a sensitive face and compellingly clear blue eyes, but wears a slightly distant look, as though his thoughts are far away. Luke says the benefits system should be used as a mechanism for easing people into independence rather than, as at present, a weapon to coerce them into insecurity.

'I'm not in formal employment. I'm on my own. Since my early twenties, I suffered from mild depression. It remained mild while I was young. But in 2002, I split up with my girlfriend after a ten-year relationship. It was a great shock. I didn't see it coming. She threw me out of the flat, and I became a rough sleeper for two years.

'I slept mostly in hostels, especially the Salvation Army. It was June when I left my partner, so for a few months I slept outside. My parents said I was old enough to look after myself, and I got no help from my sister.

'It was all right during the summer. I had been working as a leather currier, a skilled job. I left to go to another firm, because the supervisor bullied me. I'd had enough. After a few months, the company I had joined went bankrupt. The firm I worked for originally is still going, but I couldn't go back there, because I had broken my loyalty, and in any case, there was still animosity towards me.

'So I was not working. While I slept rough, I think survival took over and I didn't think too much about things. It was afterwards, when I got my flat in 2004, I became severely depressed. Maybe it was delayed shock of breaking up my relationship, and exposure to all the humiliation you face as a homeless person. I went to my GP, and saw a community psychiatric nurse. I was referred to a psychologist and then to a psychiatrist. I still see the community nurse.

'Depression is a continuous psychological state. It also affects you physically. It makes you withdrawn, it changes your mood, makes you unpredictable, disturbs sleep patterns. It colours your whole perception of life. It is not the same thing as being clinically depressed.

'My father suffered the same thing – there is a history of it on his side of the family. I mean, everyone gets depressed, it is part of the normal circumstances of life; but persistent depression is a disability. It is hard to describe. In my case, it was an underlying condition, triggered by events. It was controlled as long as life was even and predictable; but a crisis exacerbated it.

'I had no long-term relationship after we broke up. My life was unreal. I was in the Salvation Army hostel in Birmingham. They fed me. I had a bed. Many of the people there were in the same position; some were a lot worse. You can't work if you have no place to live; and as an address to apply for jobs, the Salvation Army is no recommendation. It affects everything. Insecurity and anxiety eat you up. To be among people who have lost all expectation of improvement, who have lost family, have no living relative, is bad; to be among those who have lost hope is indescribable.

'Until then, I had had a relatively normal existence. I didn't leave home until I was 26. That protected me to some degree. The family background was stable. I had been moderately educated. But society as a whole is generally not sympathetic. You hear it in the words of politicians: they give licence to ignorance and prejudice. People have a fear of mental illness – fear of the unknown. Maybe they also think it is contagious. I have two friends diagnosed with schizophrenia. I know their history and it isn't a problem. But if you haven't experienced it yourself, it's hard to convey to others. Like being destitute, it is something I'll never forget. The memory of being an outcast is always there; and it comes back when you are at your most vulnerable.

'My father is in a care home. He has Parkinson's. My mother lives alone in Cannock; my sister has her own family in Bridgnorth. When I came out of being homeless in 2004 and moved into my flat, my father lost his business. He also had a breakdown and was sectioned. He had a shop, selling domestic items and electrical goods. The taxman got him. He lost everything. I have always been close to him: there are affinities in families: if you resemble them, you feel closer to them.

'There are things that alter your life, whether for good or bad. You can't anticipate them. In my case, depression completely restructured the way I think and the way I live. I have been under pressure from the Jobcentre. They can be very unsympathetic. Now I am on Employment and Support Allowance. I don't know what happens next. Of course I want to work; but what is the government doing to overcome the prejudices of employers?

'My father was always a socialist, an old-fashioned left-winger. I grew up to think the same way. I was lucky, because at school my teachers told me it was all right to have radical views, to question the way things are. That is also part of who I am – if you have been through an experience that sets you apart from people, it often makes you uncomfortable with what everybody takes for granted; and then you start asking why and when and how.'

Alison: the loneliness of being on benefit

Alison is in her mid-fifties: a woman whose pleasant manner and smart appearance give little indication of the suffering beneath. On the walls of her comfortable flat are pictures of her family – many of them now dead or lost – and photos of her cat, her main companion. Alison feels defeated. She nursed her husband for ten years until he died in 2001. He had no pension. Partly as a result of her bereavement, an older experience of depression has recurred. 'I can't work for health reasons. As well as depression, I have a stomach disorder, and psoriasis which, when it comes out, is disfiguring and so painful I cannot bear to have any clothes near it.'

The Department for Work and Pensions has told her she should work. She looked after her husband from when she was still in her thirties. He had three strokes, each one worse than the one before. They had no insurance. When he died, Alison was still under 45, and missed out on a widow's pension – what later became bereavement allowance – by two years. She got £22 a week for the 12 months after he died. She couldn't hold a job, immobilised by psoriasis. She was in and out of hospital with this auto-immune condition, linked both to arthritis and depression.

'I'm getting £150 to £160 a fortnight. Being poor only makes all other misfortunes worse. My son died recently, a heart attack at 40. As a result, I also lost my grand-daughter, who has been adopted by people who live on the south coast. My father also died of heart problems when he was 60. There has always been that weakness in the family.

'Being on benefit is hard and degrading. I've only ever had one holiday in my life, and I am nearly 60. I went to Spain once with my son. The benefits officer said everyone should have one holiday a year. He said "Why don't you save up one pound a week?" How far would that get me? Your income is squeezed all the time. The rent has gone up, and I have to pay something towards council tax. I'm lucky if I have £10 a week for food.

'I also have to pay the bedroom tax. I can't afford it. I don't care if they put me in prison; at least I'd get shelter and three meals a day. I don't care anymore; that is how I feel inside. My son looked after me. He was receiving severe disability allowance, but when I had no electricity, he gave me the money to heat one room. It is all much worse when you are on your own. I've no one to turn to now. I have to carry all my burdens alone. I pop pills all day – I take Prozac and sleeping tablets. Sometimes I feel suicidal.

'When my husband died, I received no help at all. I nursed him and I nursed my other son, who is also ill, schizophrenia and manic depression. He has dementia, and has been in a residential home for the past 15 years. He comes here on Saturdays. It's company. Just having someone here.

'Loneliness is the biggest killer. I have no real communication with anyone. I have one sister much older than I am. She looks after her husband, who has Alzheimer's. My three brothers are workaholics – all they think about is work and money. I looked after them when they were small, because our mother was taken to a mental hospital when I was nine. One brother went in the army and another worked as an electrician. They took care of me until our mother and father had gone; after that, they stopped. My mother was a permanent invalid. One day, I remember, my father tried to kill himself. That was when gas could kill you. We had gone to bed. My brothers were asleep. I could smell gas. I got up and found my father unconscious, with his head in the gas oven. I broke the window and called an ambulance, and they got him to hospital.

'If I sound angry and bitter, this is because I am. I can't go anywhere. If I take the bus, it costs £4 a day for the fare. If I were fit, I'd walk, but I also have mobility problems.

'We are an unfortunate family. My mother lost her first son when he was five years old. Now I have lost my first-born. History repeats itself. Of course, poverty aggravates it. Some people have killed themselves over benefit cuts. The rich don't understand.

'With our benefits being cut, I feel like I've been robbed. I was robbed of housing: I had been living with my son who died, but then I had to move out of the house. It was too much: his girlfriend, Ella, didn't do a lot, because she is bipolar. Then Social Services took the child away. I can say without exaggeration that my heart is broken. Every night I think "Let God take me in my sleep, I have nothing to live for."

'Without money, you can't do anything. I would love to go to Birmingham to look round the shops. Stop off and have a cup of coffee. It sounds pathetic, but it's true. I have only used my washing machine once since I've had it, because I am afraid of using electricity and hot water. I have a bath only once a fortnight, the rest of the time, I wash down. I should be having two baths a day because my skins risks getting infected with the psoriasis.

'I'm a proud person. But I feel that all through my life, I've had everything taken away from me – my mother, my first son, my other son and now my granddaughter. When I was young, I wanted to be a model. I was pretty. It was my ambition to model for a clothing catalogue. And now I'm threatened with court and being left without a roof over my head. And I can't do anything about it.

'When I was a child, my mother used to say to me "When you are old enough to meet a nice man, you'll marry and settle down." The one I got was a swine. He was a drinker and he used to knock me about. I divorced him while the children were still young. I was with him eight or nine years. My second husband was a lovely man. He was a twin, but ever since birth his heart had been weak. He had seizures at times throughout our married life. I often thought he would die. I was with him the same amount of time I was with my first husband. Two different worlds.

'I had a house then, which I prefer. In flats, you are enclosed. My cat is my chief companion. If it died, I think I would kill myself. My cat is my life … Do you mind if I smoke? I stopped smoking, but the day my son died, I smoked ten cigarettes. I was violently sick. I shouldn't. I have asthma and have to use an inhaler.

'All my ailments are genetic. My father worked all his life as a long-distance lorry driver. He never claimed a penny from the State. People in the street who were better off used to offer us things, but he wouldn't take anything from anybody. We had a piano in the living room. My father sang in the choir. My brother's daughter has inherited his love of music. I don't know where my brother lives ... I take after my father ... Anyone down and out he would offer a meal.

'I have been in a psychiatric hospital with depression. I have Income Support and sickness benefit. I applied for a Personal Independence Payment. [This was refused in the first instance. It then went for 'mandatory recommendation', which means that the Department for Work and Pensions will reconsider its decision, before an appeal to a tribunal can be made. There is no time limit on this process.]

'I did have a boyfriend after my second husband died. He was younger than I. He was a great help. But we drifted apart, after eight or nine years. That seems the length of time my relationships last. It was when I was nine that my mother was taken away ... My boyfriend saw his sister die. She left a child of four. After that, we moved apart.

'People tell you that life is what you make it. It isn't. It is mostly what happens to you, especially if you have inherited disabilities. I had chronic psoriasis as a baby. I also had it when the children were small. I take diazepam to make me relax and to help me find sleep.

'It seems my family is living under a curse ... It's a funny thing, but a gypsy did curse me. One day, I was crossing a busy road with my children and our dog. I was walking slightly ahead of them. Suddenly I heard the screech of the brakes of a lorry and a scream. Before I could turn round, I cried out "Don't let the children die, let it be the dog." The gypsy heard me and cursed me. She was a real gypsy. They looked after horses in the fields. I have often wondered if I have been living under that curse.

'I believe in God. I believe in life after death. I have seen people who have died, who have come back. A boy who died on the railway came to see me. And a week before my mother died, she swore she saw my father sitting on the end of her bed. "He's come for me" she said. I believe you go to a better life when you die. That has been my only comfort. I also nursed my father before he died. He had cancer of the pancreas. I was 26 or 27 … The time when I needed him most.'

Alison has had counselling, but she didn't continue with it. She rarely goes out. In the long, lonely hours, she tells over the loss and suffering of her life, which have become, to some degree, her identity. Benefit 'reforms' can only add to her unhappiness, which they duly do. Is this a predictable result of government action, or merely a by-product of ideologically driven 'policy', from the consequences of which those who implement it are carefully shielded, both by their wealth and by a set of beliefs which, in their way, are as fanatical as those of any religious zealot?

Alison was the most deeply unhappy person I met. Even if she had not felt herself persecuted by an unforgiving system, this would probably have made little difference to her underlying feeling about life, and would, of course do nothing to alter her experience of loss. But it might have provided her with modest space for a less cramped existence, and the possibility that she might diminish *the pain of being*, which scarcely needs gratuitous augmentation from those elected to govern us, which they do by the light of a meagre and fading wisdom.

Kenneth Lennox

Some of the most dramatic stories are publicised in the press: Dawn Amos died on the day her Personal Independence Payment application was rejected. The Department for Work and Pensions wrote telling her she did not fulfil the criterion, even for the lower rate of payment. Her husband found the letter two days after her death.

These tragic extremes illuminate the crudeness and insensitivity of the system. The great majority of those caught up in the benefits system do not make headlines. It is the ordinariness of most people who feel diminished and slighted by an institution designed to relieve them of poverty without fanfare, preserving both dignity and humanity. People speak of being slighted, disbelieved, infantilised in their dealings with functionaries of the welfare state, which, having been once the preserve of 'the caring professions', is increasingly regressing into eighteenth-century 'poverty farming', when the administration of the Poor Law was also outsourced to private entities. The failure of that experiment has done nothing to dent the government's conviction that its own experiments are both bold and innovative. They aren't. They are of a piece with ancient and discredited practices.

Kenneth is 29. He wears a suit and tie, and carries a briefcase and umbrella: symbols of self-respect, and an announcement to the world that he will not be demoralised by the indignities heaped upon him as an unemployed man.

He describes himself as 'a full-time father on benefit'. He is separated from the partner he was with for three years. They have two children: the boy lives his mother, while Kenneth looks after his six-year-old daughter. He says 'Because I am on benefit, I get tarnished by those the government describes as shirkers.

'You are being dictated to all the time. If you don't do this, you won't get that. You have to make 25 job searches online in a week. I can do it because I am computer literate. Otherwise,

I'd be sanctioned. I do it through Universal Jobmatch, the government website. You log in, enter your password and your email ID. That also helps them check up on you, to make sure you have made the required number of applications. I feel sorry for people who can't use or don't have a computer. They get a double punishment, because they are made to feel they can't function in modern society. It is very demoralising. You apply for jobs and hear nothing. Some of the jobs advertised don't give any contact details. Some are duplicates. Others don't exist.'

Kenneth has been a support worker, a care assistant, a cleaner. He worked in a care home for the elderly, and assisted adults with learning difficulties. The longest job – support worker – lasted a year. He grew up without contact with his father, who left home when he was three. His mother brought up the children – three boys and a girl – on her own; but at least the State helped her, and she did not have to face the obstacles confronted by today's single parents.

The work of Jobcentres has also been downgraded. Kenneth goes there now just to sign on. 'They just put you in the Work Programme. Previously at the Jobcentre you would see an adviser, who would help you with a job search, and sort out problems with benefits. Now they don't provide any of that. It is as if they had washed their hands of you. You are on your own.

'I get Jobseeker's Allowance, now £120 a fortnight. Out of it you have find everything, and you're constantly robbing Peter to pay Paul. Our meals depend on what is in the cupboard or the freezer. My daughter likes beans on toast, which is cheap and nourishing, but you can't have that every day.

'I have a two-bedroom flat. The housing benefit is paid directly to the housing association, and that is £99 a week, including the service charge for the maintenance of the block.

'All I want is a decent job that I can fit around my daughter's schooling. I left school at 17. I did one year in the sixth form, a pilot course in leisure and tourism, but no qualification came of it. My first job was as a part-time cleaner at Asda.

'Life is a constant humiliation. You go for a job, they demand experience. I have been doing voluntary work, I have skills in administration, I meet all the criteria for job search, and I am gaining new skills in my volunteering. It isn't fair. I am being punished for those who do take advantage of the system. People who have been doing it for years know how to play the game. Even if their benefits are sanctioned, they apply to the Hardship Fund. There are ways round it when you know how.

'The last job I had was store janitor for Sainsbury's. That involved cleaning the floors, clearing up spillages – sugar, broken bottles of anything from jam to pickles. I did that for two months. I finished it because of problems with child care. You can't leave a six-year-old at home on her own. I knew what it was to be without a father. It is not going to happen to her.

'I have had interviews for sales jobs, which depend on commission. I can't do that. If you don't know from one week to the next how much you are going to earn, the benefits system cannot react to such fluctuations.

'I am not a worrier, but it tests my patience. Because I had an absent father, it made me determined to be there for my child. I will get my life sorted, but she is my priority. It's pointless getting upset about the government. I just don't believe anything they tell me. When they say things are getting better, the economy is improving – my life isn't, and that is what matters to me.

'I think the greatest injustice is when they do things that affect my daughter, cutting benefits when I have done nothing wrong. To do 25 searches in a week is impossible. I resent my daughter being punished by the State.

'If you miss one signing on, you'll be sanctioned. I have to sign on every two weeks. After two years, it will be every day. The people you deal with seem to think everybody is the same. Some talk to you decently, others just demand to see your job search, and then it's just, more or less, "bugger off".

'Last year my benefit was cut. At the end of each financial year, there is a review. They send you a form, and you have to fill in every detail of your life. It is insulting. They want to know everything, and then, at the end of it, they shave so much off your benefit. Last year, I was getting £140. I was offered no reason why a cut is justified. The only information you get is that child tax credits go down as the child gets older.

'At Sainsbury's I was worse off. I was having to pay a certain amount towards the rent and council tax, I was paid only once a month and that meant £400 every four weeks, plus tax credits. In total, I now get £120 a fortnight, £20 child benefit and weekly tax credit, which brings it up to £280 a fortnight. I was getting a winter allowance, but that has stopped. I got Surestart vouchers for fruit and vegetables, worth £2.30 a week, and also for milk. All that stopped when my daughter turned five. Until that time I was on what was called Income Support; but when she turns five you must seek work.

'How much would I need to feel secure? £300 a week minimum. Then I could pay rent, council tax, food and bills. I have debts, some of them long term. After I lost my job, the

Trustee Savings Bank extended my overdraft. Even once I'd gone onto benefit, they let the debt mount up and then passed it on to a debt-collection agency. I was threatened with court, but the costs of recovery would be greater than the debt itself. I owe about £3,000. The debt-collection agencies use threats. They can't come into your house unless you let them in. If you phone them and say you are denying them access, they are trespassing if they try to enter. There are non-violent ways of going about things, but you have to know what bailiffs can and cannot do.

'There is no point in losing your temper with officials. Once you do that, they've got you. I don't ask for much, but I don't intend to let myself be harassed by anyone.'

A number of people said they felt they were being criminalised through their poverty. 'You are made to feel you are not a full citizen of your own country.'

Marie Fullerton

Marie is 48. A small, energetic woman, she explained to me that she ceased growing at the age of 14. It was as though she felt it necessary to account for herself, as she has no doubt had to do to many welfare officials over the years. She suffers from a bone disease diagnosed only in early adulthood. 'At the age of 20 I went for tests. I had always been bullied because I was small. I had a full body scan, and then it was discovered my growth had stopped six years earlier. By that time, it was too late to repair the damage. I used to see the school nurse, and she always said I would sprout up suddenly. But it didn't happen.' It is easy to imagine how Marie must have suffered as a teenager – all who are set apart in one way or another are liable to be mocked or bullied by others. Most young people are insecure in adolescence, and readily find in solidarity against difference a consolation for, and diversion from, their own sense of anxiety.

When the government began its campaign against 'benefit cheats', its rhetoric appeared to spare those who suffered from genetic afflictions and other conditions over which they had no control. Emboldened by public approval, it seems the government is now extending its power to punish to the very people to whom charity and forbearance are due – those with disabilities difficult to remedy, or those with inherited conditions over whom reduced life-expectancy hovers like a malignant fate foretold.

Marie's family have never survived to any great age within living memory, since there is also a history of heart disease and cancer. She herself had a hysterectomy when she was 32. 'I would love to work. I hate to sit about. I am not one to do nothing.' She also has osteoporosis, and her bones can break without her being aware of it until afterwards.

'The condition comes from my father's side. My sister died of cancer. She was 57. My mother died of the same thing 11 years ago. I lost my father when I was eight. So I have known the meaning of grief and loss. It makes you wonder what life has in store for you. It is a good thing you don't know; but you can't help thinking about it; and that doesn't give you much reassurance.'

Marie's husband, Geoffrey, has a crumbling spine. In spite of this, he has just found a part-time job, delivering pizza from Chunky Grill, which he can do in his car, specially adapted to his disability. He works evenings, 16 hours a week. He says 'It is hard to work, because once you start to earn, you lose more of your benefits than you can replace.' Geoffrey had been on Employment and Support Allowance, but this was stopped when he started work. The allowance has been transferred to Marie who is awaiting a review of her case.

I have a composite memory of sitting in people's houses in the winter of 2014/15. It is always cold. At best, on cold evenings, they turn the heating on briefly, 'to take the chill off the room'. Rugs, blankets, sleeping bags, sweaters and hot water bottles were used to keep the cold at bay; talk condensed with each breath, and the cold crept up like a paralysis from feet to knees to body. It is not that most houses are uncomfortable, although many are poorly furnished. Most have a sofa and chairs, a coffee table – not a dining table, because people do not 'dine', but survive on improvised snacks, picnics and occasional take-aways: eating is functional and not necessarily time-dependent. But the lack of warmth makes everywhere cheerless. It is as though people's presence is only temporary, even when they have nowhere to go and no appointments to fulfil. This is living; permanently in something less than ease and far short of comfortable. There is little ornament in the houses of young people. Older generations often have a collection of pottery houses, china, dolls and plastic flowers. Younger families usually have a set of family photographs, often in frames – a kind of shrine to kinship, where faded grandmothers stand behind wedding photographs, and children who have lost their milk teeth smile cheekily in school photographs against a sky-blue background.

Marie says 'If you lose ESA, you have to pay something towards the rent, and a proportion of council tax. We are also liable to bedroom tax, but because of our circumstances, that has been reduced to £9 a week.

When Geoffrey was assessed for work capability, the woman in the medical centre said because he could push himself in his wheelchair 500 yards, he was fit for work. He is earning £104 a week, and his disability allowance is £89 a month. 'It would be more, but they stop me £200 a month for the car.' Marie gets £113 a week.

Their finances are extremely complicated. Many people simply do not know how the DWP calculates their income. They are only aware of fluctuations (usually reductions), and find it hard to disentangle its component parts. Marie and Geoffrey are paying back a budgeting loan to the DWP.

'We switch off the heating till late at night. I am supposed to have a special diet, because of my condition, but we can't afford to stick to it. We had debts, five or six thousand. We went to Citizens' Advice and got a Debt Relief Order.' [This is available to people owing less than £15,000, if you have a small income (less than £50 a month 'spare income'), and do not own your own home. Creditors cannot recover money without going through the court, and within 12 months the debts are 'discharged'. You cannot get a DRO if you are guilty of 'careless or dishonest behaviour', for instance, if you lied to get credit. It can be obtained only with the help of an authorised money adviser and costs £90.]

'If the debt is obviously unpayable, the slate is wiped clean after 12 months. We just got deeper into it. Loan companies are willing to lend to anyone, they encourage you. And then, there are things everybody has, and you think "Oh we could get that." But sometimes you take loans just for living – to pay heating bills or to buy food. After the 12 months is up, and the debt is cancelled, you can get no credit for six years. That's a good thing, because we don't want to get into that mess again.

'The people they send to collect the debts scare you. They're constantly calling, or knocking at the door. One man really frightened me. I am a worrier anyway, but this particular one came to the door, and I said to him my husband was not in. "Come back in an hour." He said "No, you'll get the money now. Get it from a friend or a neighbour." He stuck his foot in the door, which they are not allowed to do. I was in a state of constant anxiety over all the money we owed.

'We have lived here about five years. I have three children, one from my first partner, and two with Geoffrey. Samantha is 28, Tania 23 and Mark 21. The younger two are both care workers. Mark has just got engaged to a nursery teacher and has moved in with her – that's why we have to pay bedroom tax. My daughter's partner works as a salesman. They've all done well and we're proud of them.

'When the children are growing up they put pressure on you to get things. They don't want to feel left out. The girls especially, as teenagers, have to have what other people do. For me, it was a priority to make sure my children didn't want for anything. We are close. When we say goodbye we always tell each other "I love you". I was lucky, because I had a very loving mother.

'Geoffrey went off with a woman at one time, but it didn't last. She was the kind of woman who made a habit of breaking up marriages. There are some people who need to show that they can get anybody they want; and once they've done it, they lose interest. In the end, she didn't want him, so he moved back.

'I went with a chap when I was 18. He knocked me about. He was nice when I met him, but when he started drinking, he couldn't keep his hands to himself. He would kick and punch me. I'm very soft, I wouldn't hurt a fly. That also brings out the bully in some people. You think domestic violence is a thing of the past, but I know plenty of women who are still scared of their husbands. I haven't got a bad bone in my body. If you are soft-hearted you get taken advantage of. My attitude to life is "Enjoy it, because you only come this way once." I believe this is all there is. Once this life is over, that's it – you go back to where you came from.

'I have one grandson. He is 11 months old. I look after him every Thursday and that is the highlight of my week. I love him to bits.'

A majority of people face the circumstances of their life with fortitude. To impose upon them an ideology designed to make them change their behaviour mocks their struggles.

Gus: a heroic life

Gus lives in a two-storey block close to the city centre. His flat is well-maintained, decorated in black and white – a white rug, white leather chairs, a black glass table – a taste Gus is proud of. In his late fifties, he is amiable and easy-going, and talks with engaging frankness. He says he is liable to pay the bedroom tax, but 'because of my financial difficulties' this has been waived. He has lived here for many years, a well-recognised figure in the neighbourhood. His life has been almost eighteenth-century in its picaresque adventures and sexual excitement. He is positive and defiant, a survivor.

He and his present woman friend live apart. 'I like to be with her for a couple of hours, but don't want to spend too much time in her company. I have a lot of Sikh friends in the neighbourhood – nothing I like better than a bowl of curry which I eat together with them, a laugh and a joke.

'My woman friend is Muslim. I used to be the biggest racist bastard in the world. I was in the National Front. I couldn't stand blacks or Pakis or anyone who wasn't like me. I was brought up on a predominantly white estate, where it was natural to be racist. It's what you grow up with. That is, until I started talking to people.

'I met her in a pub. She was drinking Coke. Her brother and her sister and their kids all love me. They call me "Granddad", because their real grandfather split from his wife. I've met all the aunties and uncles – they call everybody auntie and uncle, even if they are no relation. It's a great life. She doesn't go to mosque, but she prays at home. It opens your eyes to what family means.

'I think relations between the races are improving. At the end of the day, why be racist? We've all got to live together, you might as well make the best of it. When I had to go into hospital, I put myself down as a white Muslim, so I got all the curry meals.

'My first wife and I divorced. We had two kids. She still lives on the Heath Town Estate. I split up with my second, because she was always running away. I couldn't leave her, even for half an hour, because if I did, she'd be gone by the time I got back. She went to refuges, hostels, boarding houses in Birmingham, Bristol, London. She couldn't settle. We ran a hotel in Tenby for two years, but even there, she was always taking off. If I went out, by the time I got back, she would have taken everything she could carry, gone off in a taxi.

'I haven't seen her for 20 years, but I'm still married to her. She took the baby. I never knew why she left, she couldn't say.

She'd come back and say "Let's start again." But the same thing happened. She never went back to her family. I wanted to get a divorce, but nobody could find her. One day she stabbed me; another time, she broke my jaw. I was in bed, having a curry, and I said to her 'I'd like some bread and butter with it.' She went out and when she came back, she had a knife in her hand and stabbed me. The police came. They knew her. The babby stayed with me till her family took it. She is now grown up, gone the same way her mother did.

'If I include all my step-children, I must have 23 or 24 kids; only one child with the one I'm still married to. I had a baby with one girlfriend, who brought the little girl to my house one day and said "Here is your daughter. Can you look after her for a couple of hours?" She went back to her mum's house and they went off to Spain. I kept the child for five years. After that, I took ill. I phoned her mum and stepfather and asked them to take her. She is 12 now. A lovely girl. She was born the same year my mum died. All the time I was looking after her, she came first. I love her.

'I'm 56 now. I've had plenty of women. At Yates's [wine lodge] they are good to me. "Here he is", they say, when I go in. They have a party on my birthday, karaoke, costs me nothing.

'I've got a rare lung disease. I have gone down from 18 stone to nine stone. There's only three other people in this country who've had it, and two of them are dead. It came on suddenly. I was walking along one day, and was sweating, couldn't get my breath, felt giddy. They didn't know what it was. I had an AIDS test, but was clear. I went to Heartlands Hospital in Birmingham, and the specialist said to me "Have your last cigarette now, before the operation." I still smoke, but less. My lungs had stuck to my ribs. They cut me open and had to cut the lungs away from the rib-cage.

'I get infections easily. I still can't breathe. I get knackered, just walking a hundred yards. It's been 30 years, and it isn't going to get any better. I get mouth ulcers, and as they disappear, holes appear in my lungs. If I have a couple of pints I can walk a bit further.

'When I was young I had a lot of jobs – roofer, foundryman, fork-lift truck driver, I worked in the building trade. I don't do much now, a few bits and pieces. I take painkillers all the time. I'm on warfarin. That's another problem – my blood thickens and then it goes too thin. That's all down to the lung disease. I also have a heart monitor, but that's got too old to be of any use. They are going to replace it.' Gus has a small black box, which he must carry with him everywhere, because the heart monitor will automatically communicate with the hospital 'if I pass out'.

'I used to be a professional boxer. I made money. I was a light heavyweight. I was good. A guy came into Yates's one night and says "Let me buy you a drink. I used to bet on you with your dad." He had made money out of me. I was rated number six in Britain in that category in my twenties. Even today, nobody messes with me.

'They tried to get me over the bedroom tax. But if my friend Mariam comes over, or the kids, I've got to have a room for them to pray in. I have two kids with her. They are my Indian family and I am proud of them.

'I should be dead by now, but I'm still here. To me, if you want to be sad, that's your problem. I want to go out and have a laugh. I've loved the women. "Get in the bedroom and get your knickers off" is my outlook. Anything bad, I'd rather not know. It's like cancer. Years ago, people never knew if they had it. If you do know, what are you going to do about it but worry? The worry will kill you off before the cancer does. I was so ill at one time, I was given only weeks to live. I looked at myself in the mirror, I saw my eyes sunk and cheeks pale, and I started fighting back.

'My mother died of a blood clot. She felt tired, went to bed and died. My father died of cancer of the gullet. I'm not bothered about dying. I've had my fun, my good days. I'm not going to give in. If I die, I die, but that won't stop me doing what I want to do. When your time comes, that's it. I don't know anything about life after death, because nobody has ever come back to tell me about it. To me, you're born on this earth and you might go to a better place. You pray to God or Allah or any other god, but nobody has ever seen them.

'I have two sisters and three brothers. Some I get on with, some I don't. My own children have done well – construction, one does landscape gardening, one has a café, another is a prison psychologist.

'I did love Sandra, the woman I'm still married to. And Delia, who I married first. But the two I'm closest to are Mariam and Amina – they are both Muslims. I call Mariam my knockabout. I'm closest to her. My niece and my sister don't like her, but if I'm sick she comes and brings me food. She's golden. I'm soft-hearted when it comes to women.

'They sent me to Birmingham for a medical to see if I was fit for work. He was a foreign doctor, I couldn't understand him. Two months later, they sent for me again. This time she was a Jamaican. She said "I've read your file. You'll never be able to work again." They still sent someone from the DWP, who said

"Can you do a bit of work?" I said "Are you daft or what?" I never heard anything else.

'I've been here eight years. I like it. There is a problem with the woman downstairs. Her flat is full of rubbish, papers, bags, bottles, she never throws anything away. It smells. The stink comes up here. I said to her son "Do something about it." He said it was the drains. Then the woman next door complains about the smell of curry.

'I know what it means to be racist. But I also know how much better life can be when you mix with all the people there are from different parts of the world.'

Gus brushes off the obstacles the system places in his way. If he is not going to be perturbed by the fragility of his own life, he is not going to concern himself about the benefits system. Life is too full to be overwhelmed by the unwelcome attentions of government, at least for people who enjoy networks of support, generosity and ingenuity. Those who, like Gus, know how to attach people to themselves, flourish even if they are sick. He improvises, is resourceful and not easily intimidated.

Stolen identities: epitaph for a working class

Stories of stolen identities circulate – credit cards, National Insurance numbers, driving licences, passports, diplomas: this is a metaphor that taunts these former industrial towns and cities. Their purpose was the labour required to serve staple industries; the identity of 'worker' required no elaboration, since it permeated every aspect of life – the tramp of boots on the pavement in the chill morning, the phalanx of cycles leaving the factory at dusk; factories, forges and workshops that dominated each district, the pubs and music halls, bleak chapel walls and soot-encrusted tombstones in the churchyard, and the constant presence of authority figures – bailiffs, overseers, foremen, policemen, magistrates, ministers of religion and poor-law officials.

To be stripped of this identity is like being flayed; any replacement is a flimsy covering to those who remain of this vanishing population. It is a tragedy of the death of manufacturing Britain that those whose lives were caught up in its rituals and compulsions were never permitted to grieve for its passing. There was no space for any acknowledgement that human lives were rooted here, with all the grace and sadness that accompany them. Obsessed with an ideology of progress, few have paused to ponder on the subjective experience of those whose world and whose emotions, for five or six generations, were shaped by, and rooted in, this environment, with all the sorrow, pride and pain it imposed upon them. When it was stripped away, the people became either victims of the ideology of perpetual growth, or, if they resisted, as the miners did in the 1980s, *criminals*, who stood in the way of economic necessity.

The question is not whether something better has succeeded it – the improvements are so obvious they scarcely require mention – but whether the passing of any way of life deserves an acknowledgement it has never received, particularly when it took such a toll of body and spirit on the women and men who had no choice but to make their home in the industrial wastelands.

The cries of liberation came less from the throats of the liberated than from those who stood to gain from the *demolition* of a working class; these were, unsurprisingly, the heirs and assigns of those who had profited from its violent creation in Victorian England. Reparation for this violence is a question on few political agendas.

These are not theoretical reflections. Identity has become mutable, a post-industrial fluidity of being, in which *who you are* is also a tradeable commodity, a form of shifting cultivation. Websites offer fake driving licences for as little as £20, while stolen passports command large sums; forged bank-notes permit interlopers of wealth, while money-laundering cleanses the filthiest lucre.

In an age of a faltering sense of who we are, we should perhaps not be surprised to find so many complaints of stolen identity in its many forms. The theft of credit cards which empty people's accounts; the stealing of names, licences, log-books, as well as forged documents; people pretending to be someone they are not (scams from the widows of former finance ministers of Gambia who have a mysterious urge to share their fortunes with you); the manufacture of fake money, labels, brands, medicines, garments, accessories; the dealing in contraband; the profit to be got from appearances by the quick-change artists, con-men and women; the fly-by-night builder and the quack; the dealers in goods at giveaway prices; adulterators of drugs and purveyors of altered states of mind; transferable numbers, registrations, tenancies, certificates of professional training – all illusions that are cheap and lucrative. Labour was, of course, always a reductive and limiting source of identity, and to liberate the humanity of those beneath this abstraction is a true emancipation. Identity become volatile and changeable is one thing; when it dissolves and evaporates altogether, it is a different matter; and a world where we no longer know who anyone is also casts doubt upon our own sense of self.

Tom, in his thirties, was badly injured in a car crash. After a long spell in hospital, he was anxious to work again. To prepare for this, he got a qualification for security work in a shop or warehouse. He was issued with a badge from the Security Industry Authority. It was cloned by someone now working in his name. Tom has no idea who it is: he signed up to an agency three years ago, never worked as security guard, but remained on their books. A letter informed him the agency no longer existed, but he thought no more of it. There is no way of checking who has been using the security badge. It is not unusual for people to clone an ID and use it to cover their traces.

Whoever is using Tom's badge does not know he is claiming benefit. The Inland Revenue have a record that he is earning. He says 'I feel my life is being taken away from me. Someone pretending they are you is disturbing. You feel insecure. It is scary. You wake up in the night and think Who am I? Somebody out there says he is you – you could be held responsible for anything he does – debt, crime, even murder.'

It is remarkable that in a society where people are subject to more surveillance than ever before – lives recorded, documented, accounted for by diplomas, degrees, qualifications and all the paraphernalia necessary for passing through the modern world – there should be so much fraud, error, false representation and impersonation. A man whose driving licence had been stolen was arrested by the police, who had evidence that he had purchased a Mercedes, and driven it from the forecourt of a showroom for a down payment only one-tenth of its value. He was held in custody until evidence was produced that he had had no part in the fraud.

Benefit fraud, too, is not simply a fantasy of a punitive government; although it is far less widespread than the government claims and people believe. A young woman had used a false passport to make a claim to which she was not entitled. She was found out, taken to court and presented with a bill of £2,000, which she was paying back at the rate of £17 a fortnight. I also met a family who, following a government invitation to do so, had denounced their neighbours for working while claiming benefit. There had been reprisals – acts of petty, sub-criminal vindictiveness – and they had to leave the area. They said 'We wish to God we had never said a word. We thought we were doing our duty. It turned into a nightmare.'

In this mutable world, even the closest ties of kinship and elective attachment fray: estrangements and separations, abscondings and disappearances show us we never really knew those we loved, or thought we loved; we had simply not discovered the full extent of the treachery and deceit of those close to our heart.

One reason why the politics of identity is dominant in our time is that the new identities are no longer primarily economic but existential: those of ethnicity, gender, sexual orientation, disability, age or religion. They cut across, and divert attention from, economic status and function, so that although certain groups are certainly more disadvantaged economically than others, the presence of some rich blacks, certain wealthy women, a number of successful lesbians and gay men, smart people who have triumphed over what were once insurmountable disabilities, also serves as a screen behind which inequality drives people further apart, and new mutations of poverty remain in shadow. It is significant that talk is now of 'equalities'. This simple use of the plural suggests that the highest vision of our 'advanced' society is now a 'fairer' distribution of widening inequality.

Just as fraud has been carried out by the 'financial industry' on a grand scale, which makes benefit crime look less than petty, so identity theft has been executed wholesale by those who have for centuries evicted whole populations out of familiar and hard-won crafts and occupations, and compelled them to make their accommodation with a changed – and global – employment structure, or to fall and be condemned as failures, losers and no-hopers, outcasts, loonies, alkies, druggies, loners, the untouchables of progress. For the sake of clarity, it is important to state that this observation has nothing to do with nostalgia, regret for the past or a romantic view of working-class life. Industrial life was harsh, violent and cruel, repressive of women and children, and exploitative of the heavy male labour on which it depended. But its passing creates ambivalences and contradictions: if its vices are all too often rehearsed, its virtues – of endurance and stoicism, of mutual help and the visibility of one's own fate in the misfortunes of others – also deserve to be rescued from the indifference of posterity, for it was out of these qualities that the welfare state was born. And it is the erasure of memory of the past that makes the work of welfare demolition easier, while preparing the way once more for who can say what declining futures, what fresh plunder and exploitation of the people. Unless, that is, the qualities of solidarity and unity in the face of adversity can be rescued from epic forgetting, which we are urged to embrace as the highest emancipation.

Conclusion

Although the focus of this book has been primarily on welfare, this cannot be detached from the wider project, of which it is only one aspect. The assault on well-being has been made possible by the worldwide spread of a system initiated by Britain (and its empire in the first era of globalisation), perfected in the USA, and now exported to virtually every country on earth. It is a globally instituted economic violence, since it sets the peoples of the whole planet in intense competition with one another. This, and the apparent extinction of alternatives, has led to the success of the powerful in setting about dismantling protections against poverty, loss and want in the richest societies on earth, in order not to lose David Cameron's 'global race'.

When majorities fail to resist pressure on the weakest and most vulnerable, there is nothing to prevent further erosion, both of our hopes for a better life and of our liberties in this imperfect one. To those who are precariously situated, it can be said 'It will be your turn next'; and to the comfortable, 'You will be future targets'; while only the super-rich, who occupy an aerial topography above geographical borders, the intangible home country of the patriots of wealth, will remain untouched.

During the nineteenth century, most government legislation (despite, or perhaps because of, a continuing fear of the poor) was designed to improve the conditions in which people lived and laboured. This was carried out in the name of 'reforms' which, prompted by popular resistance and the self-interest of ruling elites, made life more bearable, mitigated the worst effects of capitalism, and served as a civilising influence on the savagery of the free market in labour. This has been reversed in our own late, enlightened times: government now intervenes in the lives of the poor for the opposite purpose: to worsen their condition, to add to the already considerable pain of those least able, for whatever reason, to compete.

Is this government by nostalgia for the lost world of industrial and imperial supremacy, a desire to recapture for a post-industrial future the pre-eminence of the nineteenth century? Is it a kind of sympathetic magic, designed to reestablish at least some of the conditions that prevailed when Britain was the workshop of the world and its dominant global power? Or is it simply a dedication to the rehabilitation of an ideology sharply contested in the industrial age, but which may face less powerful challenges when industry has been obliterated, replaced by a techno-feudalism in which the masters of robotics, artificial intelligence and the gadgetry of informatics, communication and knowledge, lord it over people who perform tasks akin to those of agricultural labourers in the era before the industrial revolution?

Of course the realisation of that malign vision remains, for the present, a distant aspiration. For one thing, the government, while paying obeisance to non-interference in the economy, is nevertheless busy intervening in the social consequences of those inviolable economic freedoms: its concern for the obesity crisis, parenting skills, alcohol consumption, compulsory language-classes to prevent 'radicalisation', the wholesale demolition of the homes of the poor in an effort to 'end poverty', cannot be separated from the economic developments on which government constantly congratulates itself. For the time being, at least, the reduced State is highly selective in its withdrawal from our lives.

Whatever moves the occupants of 'high office', when a system of social security is detached from answering need and becomes, instead, a project for saving money, its purpose is destroyed. 'Deficit reduction' is one thing, but when that financial deficit is accompanied by a deficit of compassion and humanity, the costs are transferred elsewhere; and in the long run, these prove far greater than any sum of money saved. Eventually, of course – as has always occurred – it will dawn upon government and people alike that poverty is simply the shadow of wealth, and not caused by the moral failings of the unfortunate. The history of the Poor Law suggests periods of hard-heartedness always alternate with moments of leniency; times of blame give way to a kindlier understanding of the social and psychological reasons for why people are poor. At the moment, we are in a highly punitive phase. Just how far this will go before a change of heart takes place, it is impossible to say. At present, any diminution in severity towards the alleged wilfulness of the poor seems a long way off.

Just as in the early nineteenth century workers had not yet understood the rules of the capitalist game, so in our time we have not fully recognised the regressive intention of a world which is apparently abuzz with an excitable future of technological innovation, continuously upgraded communications systems, electronic contrivances, medical technologies to prolong life and the 'miracles' these can deliver. Perhaps resistance will become possible only when the journey back to an ideological past inflected by futuristic hi-tech iconography is more fully realised. If so, it falls to today's radicals to illuminate and to reverse that perilous journey to the past, and to assemble a majority against it. This requires more than a revival of the lapsed consciousness of an industrial labouring class. It involves an awakening from the somnambulist market-induced trance, a new alertness to the threat to humanity from events which take place under the false colours of progress, freedom and 'reform', when all social and political movement is backwards, and involves a curtailment of opportunity, a cramping of the full flowering of humanity, increased surveillance, and a diminution of liberty on a planet where climate change is blamed upon 'anthropogenic activity' – a euphemism for the lifestyle of the rich.

The people who have told their stories in this book are victims of the global restoration of a belief system which had been thought vanquished, but which has been resuscitated to lay waste systems designed to humanise it; triumphant, it now scythes through the world, demanding its tribute of flesh. It may seem odd, in the prosaic, familiar world of the everyday, as people go about the ordinary business of shopping, travelling, working and enjoying themselves, that a form of human sacrifice should be practised with such self-righteous savagery. The people who formulate the policies knowingly inflict hardship upon those less fortunate than themselves, in the interests of restoring a capitalism which – so they calculate, perhaps accurately – with its global power will sweep all before it for the foreseeable future: not only humanity, exhausted in its relentless service, but perhaps also the debris of a planet which its sacred laws will have reduced to ash and cinders.

Marx once deplored the efforts of philosophers who merely sought to understand the world, when the point was to change it. At that time, the nature of the change required was all too apparent. But when the world is no longer as intelligible as it was in the fume-filled light of the industrial furnace, advocacy of change is bewildering, particularly since constant change is the principal weapon of those whose main objective is the conservation of nothing but wealth and power.

In a celebrated remark in the 1848 *Communist Manifesto*, Marx stated: 'What the bourgeoisie produces, therefore, above all, is its own gravediggers. Its fall and the victory of the proletariat are equally inevitable.'

In one of the great ironies history – that melancholy and unreliable instructor – has produced, it appears that the proletariat, far from being the gravediggers of capitalism, seek nothing more than to feast at its sumptuous banquets, increasingly within reach of its outstretched arms. The gravediggers of capitalism – indeed, of all social and economic systems – are those who use up the resources of the world at an accelerating pace; people universally admired precisely for their wealth, the consumers of the substance of the earth, the demolitionists of the planet. For as long as such people serve as a model and inspiration in the context of a globalised economy, their work of destroying the home of humanity itself will continue; and the overheating of the climate – both mete-orological and social – will bring about a ruin the lineaments of which appear each day with increasing clarity.

There is no dearth of analysis and reportage; no shortage of passion, action and commitment. What we lack is a story, a narrative as powerful as that of our opponents, to knit together dissent and struggle: a common and understandable, mobilising myth, perhaps, as strong as the capitalist fable that we can all get richer, or the Marxist story that history was on the side of the workers, or the powerful national, linguistic, religious and ethnic narratives of belonging. The Greens with their vision of a planet under threat, socialists with their insights into inequality, activists fighting the unchosen migrations caused by economic warfare, conservationists who reject the destructive effects of 'development' – all offer elements of the counter-narrative that may unite resistance. But the summons to contemporary liberation remains to be articulated.

More vibrant discussions of the future of humanity in a finite world are going on all around us, and organisations which contest not only the wretched nostalgias of Western governments, but also the equally abstruse theological exegeses of the scripture attributed to Marx, are everywhere opening up elevating debates. They may have been marginal until now, but they are today inescapably forcing themselves into the crumbling management of a system controlled and manipulated by those whose 'governance' has brought impoverishment, social strife, war and relentless change, all in the name of conserving, not the earth, but the privileges of the rich.

Further reading

Among writers on global and local crises, it is impossible to recommend too highly Naomi Klein, Susan George, Joseph Stiglitz, Thomas Piketty and Owen Jones, while Polly Toynbee and Aditya Chakraborty have been consistently sharp critics in the *Guardian*. The *New Internationalist* periodical is still going strong after almost half a century, while *Race and Class* continues its cool incisive analysis of the consequences of globalism.

Many highly readable recent publications on the present austerity policies include *Austerity Bites* (Mary O'Hara); *Against Austerity* (Richard Seymour); *Social Movements in Times of Austerity* (Donatella della Porta); *Good Times, Bad Times: The Welfare Myth of Them and Us* (John Hills); *Breadline Britain: The Rise of Mass Poverty* (Joanna Mack and Stewart Lansley; *Inequality and the 1%* (Danny Dorling); *Getting By: Estates, Class and Culture in Austerity Britain* (Lisa McKenzie).

'I'm thrilled that the Left Book Club is back on track. The original club, founded by Victor Gollancz in 1936, played a pioneering role in promoting the discussion of progressive ideas at a vital time in British, and European, history. The re-establishment and relaunch of the club comes at a vital moment in the twenty-first century, a moment I believe could be a tipping point as the world rejects neoliberal values in favour of democratic socialist ideas.'

— Mick Whelan, General Secretary of ASLEF
ASLEF represents 18,750 train drivers (96 per cent of the train drivers in Britain) with a retired members' section of 2,500.